Financially FOCUSED

A 12-Week Journal

Financially FOCUSED

Amanda Kendall, EA

Financially Focused: Daily Practices to Elevate Your Profits (A 12-Week Journal)
Published by Amanda Kendall, EA and Elevating Profits LLC
Westminster, CO

ISBN: 978-1-088-93640-5

BUSINESS & ECONOMICS/Accounting/Financial
BUSINESS & ECONOMICS/Budgeting

QUANTITY PURCHASES: Schools, companies, professional groups, clubs, and other organizations may qualify for special terms when ordering quantities of this title. For information, email
Hello@ElevatingProfits.com.

Cover design and layout by Katherine McGraw Patterson LLC

DEDICATION

To Liam and Daniel,

You two are the greatest gifts in my world and the reason I dream big. You can do anything you want in this world and I will always be your biggest cheerleader. You are the reason I pushed through the tough financial times and came out on this side of it as a better person overall. I love you both plus one always.

To Jake,

You have been my biggest supporter from day one. Always encouraging me to chase my dreams, to do the work, to be better, do better and live better. You knew this was inside of me and the first day I spoke of it you encouraged and honored the time needed to bring it to fruition. Your support and love means more than you know and for that I love you now and always.

To you,

The entrepreneur. The one who loses sleep thinking of finances. The one who works long, endless hours and sacrifices so much to follow your heart. The one who knows there is a better way. This journal is for you. These are the exact steps I took to turn my business around. Ten months with no paycheck and a loss on the books that I didn't think I could recover from to thriving in business and growing every day.

There will be hard days and there might be harder days ahead. But I promise you they are worth it. So worth every single day of the crazy and exciting roller coaster of entrepreneurship. You started this journey because you were meant to, now it is time to take control of the finances so you can continue this journey to impact every single person you are meant to and to live the life you became an entrepreneur for.

Financially focused, financially secure, freedom of time and choice. It is all yours. Go get it!

TABLE OF CONTENTS

INTRODUCTION

The finance side of business can be so tough. There are days that it will leave you on cloud nine and days it can literally take you to your knees. But if you master this side of your business, even just a little bit, it can completely change the course of your business, the life you live and the things you spend your time on. Trust me, I did just that.

I have always had a knack for numbers, even growing up, math was my jam. It was where I thrived. There was a clear right and wrong answer and only one, sometimes two ways to get to that answer correctly. It was so black and white. I loved that. There was no interpretation of right or wrong, it just was. To me this was magical. Everything in life had a gray area and was open to interpretation and that tended to make me nervous. I liked clear lines. (I have gotten better at this by the way.)

I didn't plan on being an entrepreneur, it happened by circumstance forcing me down that path a bit. I was working for a gentleman who decided he was done with his business and asked me to help him wind down his tax resolution business. I worked for him while starting my own company. I didn't see another option at that time. When he told me he was closing shop, I was around five months pregnant and just getting ready to work from home for him. Women, you can relate to trying to have someone hire you when your belly is clearly about to blow up to the size of an oversized watermelon any day. I decided at that time that I would open my own business. I loved what I did, I knew a lot of people and I had made a reputable and good name for myself in the short (comparative) time I had been in the industry. People knew me. People referred to me. I knew I could succeed at this. After all, the math all added up.

The first couple years were as great as they could have been. Clients came in, clients referred clients, I networked, I filled my schedule. I took a paycheck after only seven months. I thought this was miraculous. It was a small paycheck, not anything to write about (pun intended) but it was a paycheck. This was now, at the time this was written, seven years ago.

During that time, things took an ugly turn. I got comfortable. I stopped managing the numbers.

Business was good. Referrals were consistent. I got too comfortable. I started focusing on taking some extra time off, letting the staff handle more. I had a partner that we parted ways, I had a big revenue source for my business just disappear, quite literally overnight. I made desperate choices to try and replace that revenue source, choices that almost took me out of entrepreneurship.

I realized one day, after ten months of not taking a paycheck and barely figuring out a way to make ends meet (I even delivered pizzas for several months during this time to make sure I could pay bills and feed my kids) that I needed to know why this had happened to me. In digging for an answer to that, I realized one of the biggest gut punch answers… it had happened because of me. I had let things slip. I had been mismanaging expenses, not managing revenue and the prices staff were charging were way low out of their desperation to close the sale. But I had no idea of any of this while it was all going on.

I decided right then and there to fix it. I took full control back. I put my hand back in everything for the purpose of understanding where the business was and how to get back to where it had been.

There were a few key areas that I focused on every single day to make sure I was going to recover from this. It wasn't easy, it did not happen overnight, but after a year of being extremely intentional around every dollar that came into and went out of my bank accounts, I had turned things around. 183% of a turnaround to be precise.

Over the next 12 weeks days, if you commit to the practices in this journal, you will see change in your business. You will see improvements in the finances, if you take the steps and implement them. If you are not going to implement what is in this book, you might as well just throw it in the fire and let it have some purpose for you.

A little harsh, sorry, but I believe you did not get this book, whether you bought it, or someone gave it to you, because your finances are perfect. Heck even mine aren't perfect, I still intentionally implement everything in this book, every week in my business in order to continue to have a financially sustainable and healthy business that supports my dreams in life. This is how I run my business financially, over seven years into it. It is how I started my second business and operated from day one. It is how I do business.

I wish for you to have a business that supports your goals and dreams. A business that pays you and where it is easy to see trouble with the finances well before it comes because you have a pulse on your business finances, and you know the trends and how to overcome them before they occur.

12 weeks. That's all it takes.

In the next 12 weeks you have the potential to completely change your financial circumstances. You just need to make the commitment to start.

What you do in the next 12 weeks determines the possibilities, the outcome, and your success.

Business financial goals do not need to be hard in order to succeed. In fact, I believe the exact opposite. Keep them simple, map out a clear path of success, and get to work.

Where most people get caught up is the mapping out how to get there. In this journal, I break this down to simple steps. Start with the goal and break it down to what is needed daily in order to achieve that goal.

If you follow this 12-week map to hit your goals, you will have the financial success you want for the next 12 weeks. It will require dedication, it will require focus, it will require getting out of your comfort zone, but it will be worth it.

And don't stop with just 12 weeks, use this map for every 12-week period and you will have the best financial year in business yet.

Here is to making the money that will allow you to start paying yourself regularly and consistently. Here is to the next 12 weeks. To financial success. To being a successful entrepreneur!

CFO TIME: BE THE BOSS

We have all been told at one point or another that you must work on your business as well as in your business. This includes working on the finance side also. You must designate time out of your week to look at and spend time with your finances. This should be a time of the day when you are at your best. This may be first thing in the morning, this may be in the evening, the time of day is completely up to you, but you need to block it out on your schedule and do not waiver. Honor this appointment with yourself just as you would if you had an appointment with a client. I also highly recommend this be on a normal working day for you. If you schedule this on a day that is typically your day off, then it is even more likely than it would be on a workday to get "pushed off" or "forgotten".

DAILY FOCUS

Your CFO time can be as little as a half hour a week to start. You will know best how much time you need to commit to this. What you do during your CFO time should not waiver. This is the time each week when you should be looking at the weekly finances and tracking your actual figures compared to the goals you have set. In this journal, we will do some of these tasks daily, but daily it should not take you more than 10 minutes in the morning and 10 minutes at the end of your day to fill out the daily information.

Daily Operations

1. Total Revenues brought in for the day.
    a. Did you hit your daily target?
        i. Yes- great. Give yourself a big high five.
        ii. No- What does that adjust your daily goal to tomorrow or for the rest of this week to hit your weekly goal?
2. Accounts Receivable
    a. Are the clients that should have paid you that day all paid up?
        i. No – have you had a conversation with them and scheduled payment. Don't let this go too long and don't let your clients/customers make this a habit. Set boundaries and expectations with them.
        ii. Yes- Give yourself and your staff a pat on the back.
3. Accounts Payable
    a. What bills did you pay today?
    b. Did you pay payroll or take pay for yourself out of the business?
    c. Record all the expenses and dollars that went out of your business today.
4. Calculate the daily profit
    a. Income brought in – minus expenses that went out
5. Make note of how much of the profits you are going to move to your profit/capital acount for business savings.

WEEKLY FOCUS

On a weekly basis, you should pay your bills during your CFO time. This eliminates a few minutes here and there all week long being a distraction from other income producing activities and allows you to streamline the process. Make sure you are very conscious of when invoices are due, so you are not incurring late fees, but get yourself to streamline all the bills being paid during this time.

During this time, you should be looking at your financial reports. Even if you have a bookkeeper, you still need to know how to read these, what they mean for your business and be looking at them regularly.

You should also look at your weekly revenues and expenses to make sure nothing looks out of place. Look at your goals you set for the week. Did you hit them? Did you exceed them? Did you fall short? If you exceeded the goals, the one thing you do not want to do is adjust the following weeks goals down. Keep them the same and exceed your goals for the month. If you fell short, look at why and see what you need to adjust in order to make sure you hit the target goal for the following week.

Weekly Operations

1. Once a week you should transfer the weeks savings over to the capital or profit account, so it is not sitting in your day-to-day operating account.
2. List out the anticipated sales for the following day
    a. Who have you been talking to that you need to follow up with tomorrow?
    b. Who do you need to reach out to and talk to them about becoming a client?
    c. Who are the people you need to talk to that know people that need to become your client?

YOUR WHY, YOUR WHO, AND YOUR WHAT

Several years ago, when I had to get real about how I was running my finances, it required a shift in not only my business, but my daily life. My kids had gotten used to having me around more, and I had relaxed a lot of my habits. As I started to retake control of my finances, I not only needed my boys to understand why, but I needed their support.

My kids are my WHY. After all, I started my business to provide a good life for them and our family. But, when things shifted, I also needed them to know why Mom was going to be working some late nights. They needed to know the reason Mom was pulling out the computer and paperwork during family movie time. Not only did I need them to know this may happen, but I needed them to know why.

I have never hidden finances from my kids (they are currently 12 and 7 as I write this) but I also knew I had ingrained some bad mojo about money to them and I needed to fix that also. That is why it was important for them to understand that this was important. Sitting on the other side from where I was, my kids have better relationships with money now and we budget and save as a family.

The other reason I needed them to understand what was happening is because my boys are my cheerleaders and my biggest fans. If I don't win, they lose. I needed them to understand, appreciate, and accept the changes that were happening in our family so that I could continue with confidence.

WHAT'S YOUR WHY?

First things first, though, you must know why you are pushing for this goal. What is it that makes you want this more now than you have in the past? Dig deep. Find a why so damn big that no matter what struggles come up as you are dealing with this that you will push past them because you know why you are ready now more than ever is a big one:

WHO IS THERE TO SUPPORT YOU?

Who do you need to have on board with you in order to make this goal a reality? Be specific. There are people in our lives that their support means a lot. There are people who may have to pick up more responsibility to allow us to get this part under control. There are people you may have to sacrifice some time with to get started on this. List out the people you need to get on board and then next to their name write the specific area or type of support you need from this person:

Who?	***What Kind of Support Can They Offer?***

WHAT DO YOU NEED TO SUCCEED?

What do you need to make a priority for the next 12 weeks that you may not have in the past? What are you willing to give up to achieve this goal and what are you not willing to give up? I think the not list is most important and where you should start. What are the things that cannot sacrifice during this next 12 weeks while you take control of your finances? Time with family? Sleep? Your health? List those out. Anything not on that list can be sacrificed. Maybe it is not watching your favorite TV show to have the time for this. Maybe instead of going out for drinks with friends, you make time for this. You must know those boundaries for yourself and then write them down. When you are wavering on your commitment or focus, come back and look at this page to remind yourself of the commitment you made and why. Honor that commitment to yourself.

KNOW YOUR NUMBERS

It's all about the numbers. When we're trying to get physically fit, we watch our calories: the right balance of calories in versus calories out results in a healthier body. In the same way, our financial fitness relies on watching the numbers: tracking the money that comes in and the money that goes out means healthier profits.

There are two main areas of incoming money, Income Producing Activities (IPAs) and Revenue sources. Any monies exiting your business should come in the form of Expenses. This section will help you identify the funds that are coming into and going out of your business, and help you build a budget to begin tracking those numbers on a regular basis.

INCOME PRODUCING ACTIVITIES

In order to intentionally generate profits, it is important to know what activities you engage in each day that result in revenues coming in for your business. These are called Income Producing Activities (IPA).

IPA = Income Producing Activities

This is not always just the sale.

This is the things leading up to the sale. This could be networking, phone calls, emails, social media reach outs, etc.

Take a moment and list out what your income producing activities are that you need to ensure are getting done in order to bring in revenues.

Income Producing Activities

REVENUE SOURCES

In order to be intentional with creating profits, you must know what your revenue sources are and what the average revenue from each source is.

If you have a coaching business, you might have different revenue sources as follows.

1. Book Sales
2. Online course
3. In person trainings
4. Group coaching
5. One-on-one coaching

If you have a salon yours might look like this:

1. Hair cut
2. Style
3. Color
4. Make-up
5. Product sales
6. Gift card sales

If you have an accounting business yours may look like this:

1. Bookkeeping
2. Payroll
3. Tax Preparation
4. Tax Planning
5. Business Start-up services

Whatever your business is, you most likely have more than one way that revenues are generated.

Whatever your business is, you most likely have more than one way that revenues are generated. If you don't, this is a great time to strategize how else you can bring revenues into your business, so you are not solely reliable on one source of income for your business. The more you can create multiple streams in your business, the easier it will be to engineer profits. On the next page you will list out all the ways revenue is brought into your business and what the average sale for that revenue stream is.

Revenue Source	*Average Sale*

EXPENSES

Another important piece of intentionally creating profits is managing your expenses.

I have stories upon stories where I have sat with a client and they had no idea how much money they had spent in a certain area in their business because it wasn't being monitored. The top three categories this is usually seen is meals, advertising and networking.

When you are networking or taking a client out, the meals, the coffees, it all adds up very quickly. If you are paying for one meal a day, three days a week, on average 50 weeks a year, you have paid for 150 meals as a business expense. An average meal these days will cost about $15 if you are having lunch and only paying for yourself and about $35 for a dinner. This averages at $25 per meal or $3,750.00 per year. This does not even take into account if you are having coffee meetings in addition to the meal meetings.

What would you do with an additional $3,750.00 for your business every year?

If you are not watching your expenses on a regular basis it is easy to let them get out of control.

If you are not watching your expenses on a regular basis it is easy to let them get out of con-
trol. Allowing your expenses to get out of control can have a big impact on your bottom line and without regular attention to them, they can have a bigger impact on your bottom line than you would think.

List all the expenses related to your business on the next page. Keep in mind that some may be annual, and some may be monthly; some may be fixed (like a software subscription) and some may be variable (like printing costs).

Expenses

YOUR BUDGET

One of the most important parts of this entire 12 week process is laying out a business budget. Without a budget, you don't have the start of knowing how you should be using the money in your business.

Without a budget, you don't know where you are overspending because you don't know what your spending target is.

A budget is a necessary guide on where you money should be spent in your business. Without a budget, you don't know where your money is going or how much you're spending.

A budget is not meant to dictate where you spend your money, but it is meant as a guide on how you should be spending your money in your business. When you overspend in a category consistently, it can result in you blowing your budget drastically by the end of the year. Overspending cuts into your profits, but more importantly, it cuts into what you can pay yourself.

So now it is time to lay out a budget. If you need a template for this, you can download one at ***www.elevatingprofits.com/Business_Budget*** or you can create your own template. It does not need to be anything fancy, but it does need to be something you will maintain.

If you are not sure how much you should be spending in a category, you can look at ***www.bizstats.com*** and with some digging, you should be able to find industry standards for your industry to compare to.

So put this journal down and get to work on your budget. Get this finished before you move on to the next step.

I'll wait....

Ok, now that your budget is done (because I know you are the type of person who would do the work and implement this rather than just reading and not implementing) we can move on to the next step.

SETTING YOUR PROFIT GOALS

Now that you have a budget and a clear idea of where your money is coming from (and going to), we can set your profit goal!

We're focused on your *profit,* not the revenues you will bring in. Profit can be looked at one of two ways. You need to decide which type of profit you are setting a goal for in order to accurately work these numbers.

Gross profit is the profit you make before you pay taxes.

Net profit is what you make after paying taxes on your income for the year.

I want you to be realistic but also stretch this goal a little bit to push past your comfort zone, past the success you have had in the past.

Start with history in mind. If you have been in business for a while, look at what your last year's profits were. Look at the last 12 weeks and what those profits were. Take those numbers and use as a base to set a starting point. Then from there, set where you would really like to see yourself at for the next 12 weeks.

If you are new to business, this may take a little extra work, but start with an amount of what you would like your 12-week profits to be.

CALCULATE YOUR PROFIT GOALS

What is your profit goal for this year? ....

Is this gross profit or net profit? ....

Break that out to a QUARTERLY goal (annual goal/4): ....

Break that out to a MONTHLY goal (quarterly goal/3): ....

Break that out to a WEEKLY goal (monthly goal/4.3): ....

Break that out to a DAILY goal (weekly goal/5 working days): ....

HOW WILL YOU GET THERE?

To know what you need to bring in as revenues to hit your target profit goals, we must work the numbers backwards. Let me give you an example.

Let's say you own a salon.

Your profit goal monthly is $2,500, you have expenses of $3,500, and you want to pay yourself $4,000.

To make all this happen, you need to bring in $10,000 of revenue for the month.

$2,500 +	**$3,500 +**	**$4,000 =**	**$10,000**
Profit Goal	*Expenses*	*Salary*	*Revenue*

Or, how about your accounting business?

You have a profit goal monthly of $4,000, your expenses are $2,000, and you want to pay yourself $3,000.

To make all this happen, you need to bring in $9,000 of revenue for the month.

$4,000 +	**$2,000 +**	**$3,000 =**	**$9,000**
Profit Goal	*Expenses*	*Salary*	*Revenue*

Once you have this, break it down to how many clients based on an average service price this requires you to onboard to make this happen.

Your average service price is determined by adding together all your services prices and dividing it by the number of services. Therefore, if you have a $500 service, a $1,500 service and a $4,000 service, your average service price would be calculated by dividing $6,000 ($500 + $1,500 + $4,000) by three which gives you an average service price of $2,000.

Using an average service price only works if you sell an equal number of all your products and services. An alternate way to calcuate your numbers is to figure out your sales at each price point to run these numbers rather than using an average.

For example, if you offer three services priced at $100, $500, and $1,000, and your revenue goal is $10,000, you can bring in 10 clients at your top tier, 20 clients at your middle tier, or 100 clients at your low-end.

Or, you can mix it up based on your average sales within each service category. For example, you might target three top tier clients ($3,000), 10 middle tier clients ($5,000) and 20 low tier clients ($2,000) to reach your goal.

Monthly Profit Goal: ....

Monthly Expenses: ....

Monthly Personal Pay: ....

Monthly Revenues: ....

Clients you must bring in to make this realistic: ....

***The next couple pages have been left blank for you to run various scenarios of this.

YOUR DAILY, WEEKLY, AND MONTHLY PRACTICES

You have covered your financial goal and why you want it now more than ever.

You have identified who you need to have on board to ensure you can achieve your goal and what you're willing to give up and what you are not willing to give up while achieving it.

You know what your income producing activities are and the revenue sources you bring into your business.

You have broken out your annual goal all the way to see what you need to bring in daily to achieve that goal.

Now it is time to dig into the daily and weekly practices that get you from where you are now to where you want to be in the next 12 weeks.

Ready? Let's get started!

WEEK 1

"Beware of small expenses; a small leak will sink a great ship."

Benjamin Franklin

Use your CFO time and set time aside each day to work on this journal. It should not take more than 10-15 minutes a day to keep up on this.

At the end of the week set aside an hour to spend some time looking over the week, refl ecting and setting the plan for next week.

With intention and focus on this area of your business, you will come to understand it and grow the profi ts inside your business.

TODAY'S DATE: ____________________

MY DAILY TOP 5

Five things I am grateful for about my business and business finances right now.

1. ____________________
2. ____________________
3. ____________________
4. ____________________
5. ____________________

Who do I need to reach out to today?

1. ____________________
2. ____________________
3. ____________________
4. ____________________
5. ____________________

What do I need to do today to move me forward?
What are my IPA's for the day?

1. ____________________
2. ____________________
3. ____________________
4. ____________________
5. ____________________

What do I need to learn more about today to continue to grow and deliver?

1. ____________________
2. ____________________
3. ____________________
4. ____________________
5. ____________________

Who do I need to reach out to today to make all this happen?

1. ____________________
2. ____________________
3. ____________________
4. ____________________
5. ____________________

Daily Revenue Goal:

Actual:

End of day revenues:

Number of sales:

Daily Profit:

Daily Expenditures:

Sales in the pipeline:

Daily Capital/ Income Set Aside:

TODAY'S DATE: ______________________

MY DAILY TOP 5

Five things I am grateful for about my business and business finances right now.

1. ______________________
2. ______________________
3. ______________________
4. ______________________
5. ______________________

Who do I need to reach out to today?

1. ______________________
2. ______________________
3. ______________________
4. ______________________
5. ______________________

What do I need to do today to move me forward?
What are my IPA's for the day?

1. ______________________
2. ______________________
3. ______________________
4. ______________________
5. ______________________

What do I need to learn more about today to continue to grow and deliver?

1. ______________________
2. ______________________
3. ______________________
4. ______________________
5. ______________________

Who do I need to reach out to today to make all this happen?

1. ______________________
2. ______________________
3. ______________________
4. ______________________
5. ______________________

Daily Revenue Goal:

Actual:

End of day revenues:

Number of sales:

Daily Profit:

Daily Expenditures:

Sales in the pipeline:

Daily Capital/ Income Set Aside:

TODAY'S DATE: ____________________

MY DAILY TOP 5

Five things I am grateful for about my business and business finances right now.

1. ____________________
2. ____________________
3. ____________________
4. ____________________
5. ____________________

Who do I need to reach out to today?

1. ____________________
2. ____________________
3. ____________________
4. ____________________
5. ____________________

What do I need to do today to move me forward?
What are my IPA's for the day?

1. ____________________
2. ____________________
3. ____________________
4. ____________________
5. ____________________

What do I need to learn more about today to continue to grow and deliver?

1. ____________________
2. ____________________
3. ____________________
4. ____________________
5. ____________________

Who do I need to reach out to today to make all this happen?

1. ____________________
2. ____________________
3. ____________________
4. ____________________
5. ____________________

Daily Revenue Goal:

Actual:

End of day revenues:

Number of sales:

Daily Profit:

Daily Expenditures:

Sales in the pipeline:

Daily Capital/ Income Set Aside:

TODAY'S DATE: ____________________

MY DAILY TOP 5

Five things I am grateful for about my business and business finances right now.

1. ____________________
2. ____________________
3. ____________________
4. ____________________
5. ____________________

Who do I need to reach out to today?

1. ____________________
2. ____________________
3. ____________________
4. ____________________
5. ____________________

What do I need to do today to move me forward?
What are my IPA's for the day?

1. ____________________
2. ____________________
3. ____________________
4. ____________________
5. ____________________

What do I need to learn more about today to continue to grow and deliver?

1. ____________________
2. ____________________
3. ____________________
4. ____________________
5. ____________________

Who do I need to reach out to today to make all this happen?

1. ____________________
2. ____________________
3. ____________________
4. ____________________
5. ____________________

Daily Revenue Goal:

Actual:

End of day revenues:

Number of sales:

Daily Profit:

Daily Expenditures:

Sales in the pipeline:

Daily Capital/ Income Set Aside:

TODAY'S DATE: ______________________

MY DAILY TOP 5

Five things I am grateful for about my business and business finances right now.

1. ______________________
2. ______________________
3. ______________________
4. ______________________
5. ______________________

Who do I need to reach out to today?

1. ______________________
2. ______________________
3. ______________________
4. ______________________
5. ______________________

What do I need to do today to move me forward?
What are my IPA's for the day?

1. ______________________
2. ______________________
3. ______________________
4. ______________________
5. ______________________

What do I need to learn more about today to continue to grow and deliver?

1. ______________________
2. ______________________
3. ______________________
4. ______________________
5. ______________________

Who do I need to reach out to today to make all this happen?

1. ______________________
2. ______________________
3. ______________________
4. ______________________
5. ______________________

Daily Revenue Goal:

Actual:

End of day revenues:

Number of sales:

Daily Profit:

Daily Expenditures:

Sales in the pipeline:

Daily Capital/ Income Set Aside:

WEEK 1 REFLECTION

1. Did you hit your target weekly sales goal? ....
    a. No – how does that adjust next week's goal to stay on track for the month?
    b. Yes- Have a small celebration. This is a great start.
2. Are all bills due for this week paid?........
3. All weekly transactions entered into your accounting system? ....

    This can be an actual accounting software or just a glorified check register kept in an Xcel spreadsheet, but it needs to be more than just verifying your bank account "looks right".
4. Did you pay yourself something for the week? ....
5. Did you honor your time commitment each day and at the end of the week to spend focused time on your finances? ....
6. What challenges did you face? How can you plan for those in the upcoming weeks?

    ____

    ____

    ____
7. How did those challenges impact you achieving your goals this past week?

    ____

    ____

    ____

Weekly Revenue Goal:........ Actual:........

Budgeted Expenses:........ Actual: ....

Number of weekly sales: ....

Number of sales in the pipeline for next week: ....

Weekly Profit:........

What amount did you pay yourself this week? ....

WEEK 2

Congratulations on completing the first week!

Now be honest with yourself – have you done this consistently every single day? Where did you struggle? How are you going to improve this week?

The practices in this journal are about changing old behaviors and creating new ones that will support your profit goals. You can't do the same things you've been doing and hope for different outcomes. Change isn't always comfortable, but when you see the positive results as you track your progress, you'll find it easier to stick to your new habits.

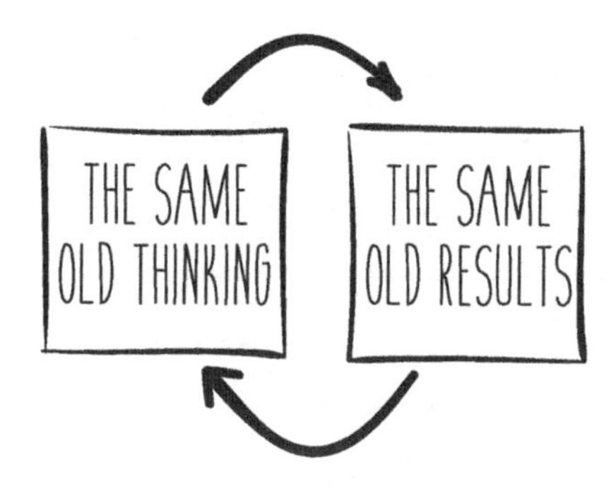

Make sure you are blocking out time on your calendar for this each day with a little extra time at week's end – honor this appointment with yourself.

Block this time out for the rest of the year on your calendar. Do this during your best time of the day when you know you will not get interrupted or distracted by anything.

TODAY'S DATE: ______________________

MY DAILY TOP 5

Five things I am grateful for about my business and business finances right now.

1. ______________________
2. ______________________
3. ______________________
4. ______________________
5. ______________________

Who do I need to reach out to today?

1. ______________________
2. ______________________
3. ______________________
4. ______________________
5. ______________________

What do I need to do today to move me forward?
What are my IPA's for the day?

1. ______________________
2. ______________________
3. ______________________
4. ______________________
5. ______________________

What do I need to learn more about today to continue to grow and deliver?

1. ______________________
2. ______________________
3. ______________________
4. ______________________
5. ______________________

Who do I need to reach out to today to make all this happen?

1. ______________________
2. ______________________
3. ______________________
4. ______________________
5. ______________________

Daily Revenue Goal:

Actual:

End of day revenues:

Number of sales:

Daily Profit:

Daily Expenditures:

Sales in the pipeline:

Daily Capital/ Income Set Aside:

TODAY'S DATE: ____________________

MY DAILY TOP 5

Five things I am grateful for about my business and business finances right now.

1. ____________________
2. ____________________
3. ____________________
4. ____________________
5. ____________________

Who do I need to reach out to today?

1. ____________________
2. ____________________
3. ____________________
4. ____________________
5. ____________________

What do I need to do today to move me forward?
What are my IPA's for the day?

1. ____________________
2. ____________________
3. ____________________
4. ____________________
5. ____________________

What do I need to learn more about today to continue to grow and deliver?

1. ____________________
2. ____________________
3. ____________________
4. ____________________
5. ____________________

Who do I need to reach out to today to make all this happen?

1. ____________________
2. ____________________
3. ____________________
4. ____________________
5. ____________________

Daily Revenue Goal:

Actual:

End of day revenues:

Number of sales:

Daily Profit:

Daily Expenditures:

Sales in the pipeline:

Daily Capital/ Income Set Aside:

TODAY'S DATE: ______________________

MY DAILY TOP 5

Five things I am grateful for about my business and business finances right now.

1. ______________________
2. ______________________
3. ______________________
4. ______________________
5. ______________________

Who do I need to reach out to today?

1. ______________________
2. ______________________
3. ______________________
4. ______________________
5. ______________________

What do I need to do today to move me forward?
What are my IPA's for the day?

1. ______________________
2. ______________________
3. ______________________
4. ______________________
5. ______________________

What do I need to learn more about today to continue to grow and deliver?

1. ______________________
2. ______________________
3. ______________________
4. ______________________
5. ______________________

Who do I need to reach out to today to make all this happen?

1. ______________________
2. ______________________
3. ______________________
4. ______________________
5. ______________________

Daily Revenue Goal:

Actual:

End of day revenues:

Number of sales:

Daily Profit:

Daily Expenditures:

Sales in the pipeline:

Daily Capital/ Income Set Aside:

TODAY'S DATE: ______________________

MY DAILY TOP 5

Five things I am grateful for about my business and business finances right now.

1. ______________________
2. ______________________
3. ______________________
4. ______________________
5. ______________________

Who do I need to reach out to today?

1. ______________________
2. ______________________
3. ______________________
4. ______________________
5. ______________________

What do I need to do today to move me forward?
What are my IPA's for the day?

1. ______________________
2. ______________________
3. ______________________
4. ______________________
5. ______________________

What do I need to learn more about today to continue to grow and deliver?

1. ______________________
2. ______________________
3. ______________________
4. ______________________
5. ______________________

Who do I need to reach out to today to make all this happen?

1. ______________________
2. ______________________
3. ______________________
4. ______________________
5. ______________________

Daily Revenue Goal:

Actual:

End of day revenues:

Number of sales:

Daily Profit:

Daily Expenditures:

Sales in the pipeline:

Daily Capital/ Income Set Aside:

TODAY'S DATE: ____________________

MY DAILY TOP 5

Five things I am grateful for about my business and business finances right now.

1. ____________________
2. ____________________
3. ____________________
4. ____________________
5. ____________________

Who do I need to reach out to today?

1. ____________________
2. ____________________
3. ____________________
4. ____________________
5. ____________________

What do I need to do today to move me forward?
What are my IPA's for the day?

1. ____________________
2. ____________________
3. ____________________
4. ____________________
5. ____________________

What do I need to learn more about today to continue to grow and deliver?

1. ____________________
2. ____________________
3. ____________________
4. ____________________
5. ____________________

Who do I need to reach out to today to make all this happen?

1. ____________________
2. ____________________
3. ____________________
4. ____________________
5. ____________________

Daily Revenue Goal:

Actual:

End of day revenues:

Number of sales:

Daily Profit:

Daily Expenditures:

Sales in the pipeline:

Daily Capital/ Income Set Aside:

WEEK 2 REFLECTION

1. Did you hit your target weekly sales goal? .... [ ]
   a. No – how does that adjust next week's goal to stay on track for the month?
   b. Yes- Have a small celebration. This is a great start.
2. Are all bills due for this week paid? .... [ ]
3. All weekly transactions entered into your accounting system? .... [ ]

   This can be an actual accounting software or just a glorified check register kept in an Xcel spreadsheet, but it needs to be more than just verifying your bank account "looks right".
4. Did you pay yourself something for the week? .... [ ]
5. Be honest with yourself, did you honor your calendared time for this task last week? .... [ ]
6. What struggles did this week bring?

   ____

   ____

   ____
7. What needs to change to go into next week set up for success?

   ____

   ____

   ____

Weekly Revenue Goal:............ [ ] Actual:............ [ ]

Budgeted Expenses:............ [ ] Actual: .... [ ]

Number of weekly sales: .... [ ]

Number of sales in the pipeline for next week: .... [ ]

Weekly Profit:............ [ ]

What amount did you pay yourself this week? .... [ ]

WEEK 3

"It's not income that makes you rich, it is your spending habits."

Benjamin Franklin

You should be getting the hang of this now. You have had this appointment with yourself every day for two weeks now. Congratulations!

This week let's put some intentional focus on where you are spending your money. The little expenses that you think are no big deal, add up, quickly. These are the expenses you need to watch closely – at the end of the year they can quickly add up to thousands of dollars.

Do you have meetings with potential clients to schedule? Maybe schedule them as a walk. Maybe take your coffee with you instead of buying the coffee on the way.

WEEK 3 MINI-CHALLENGE

This week, I challenge you to focus on the "little" expenses this week and see where you can cut out some of those to improve your bottom line.

Track those here:

Date	*Expense Category*	*Amount Saved*

TODAY'S DATE: ____________________

MY DAILY TOP 5

Five things I am grateful for about my business and business finances right now.

1. ____________________
2. ____________________
3. ____________________
4. ____________________
5. ____________________

Who do I need to reach out to today?

1. ____________________
2. ____________________
3. ____________________
4. ____________________
5. ____________________

What do I need to do today to move me forward?
What are my IPA's for the day?

1. ____________________
2. ____________________
3. ____________________
4. ____________________
5. ____________________

What do I need to learn more about today to continue to grow and deliver?

1. ____________________
2. ____________________
3. ____________________
4. ____________________
5. ____________________

Who do I need to reach out to today to make all this happen?

1. ____________________
2. ____________________
3. ____________________
4. ____________________
5. ____________________

Daily Revenue Goal:

Actual:

End of day revenues:

Number of sales:

Daily Profit:

Daily Expenditures:

Sales in the pipeline:

Daily Capital/ Income Set Aside:

TODAY'S DATE: ____________________

MY DAILY TOP 5

Five things I am grateful for about my business and business finances right now.

1. ____________________
2. ____________________
3. ____________________
4. ____________________
5. ____________________

Who do I need to reach out to today?

1. ____________________
2. ____________________
3. ____________________
4. ____________________
5. ____________________

What do I need to do today to move me forward?
What are my IPA's for the day?

1. ____________________
2. ____________________
3. ____________________
4. ____________________
5. ____________________

What do I need to learn more about today to continue to grow and deliver?

1. ____________________
2. ____________________
3. ____________________
4. ____________________
5. ____________________

Who do I need to reach out to today to make all this happen?

1. ____________________
2. ____________________
3. ____________________
4. ____________________
5. ____________________

Daily Revenue Goal:

Actual:

End of day revenues:

Number of sales:

Daily Profit:

Daily Expenditures:

Sales in the pipeline:

Daily Capital/ Income Set Aside:

TODAY'S DATE: ____________________

MY DAILY TOP 5

Five things I am grateful for about my business and business finances right now.

1. ____________________
2. ____________________
3. ____________________
4. ____________________
5. ____________________

Who do I need to reach out to today?

1. ____________________
2. ____________________
3. ____________________
4. ____________________
5. ____________________

What do I need to do today to move me forward?
What are my IPA's for the day?

1. ____________________
2. ____________________
3. ____________________
4. ____________________
5. ____________________

What do I need to learn more about today to continue to grow and deliver?

1. ____________________
2. ____________________
3. ____________________
4. ____________________
5. ____________________

Who do I need to reach out to today to make all this happen?

1. ____________________
2. ____________________
3. ____________________
4. ____________________
5. ____________________

Daily Revenue Goal:

Actual:

End of day revenues:

Number of sales:

Daily Profit:

Daily Expenditures:

Sales in the pipeline:

Daily Capital/ Income Set Aside:

TODAY'S DATE: ____________________

MY DAILY TOP 5

Five things I am grateful for about my business and business finances right now.

1. ______________________________
2. ______________________________
3. ______________________________
4. ______________________________
5. ______________________________

Who do I need to reach out to today?

1. ______________________________
2. ______________________________
3. ______________________________
4. ______________________________
5. ______________________________

What do I need to do today to move me forward?
What are my IPA's for the day?

1. ______________________________
2. ______________________________
3. ______________________________
4. ______________________________
5. ______________________________

What do I need to learn more about today to continue to grow and deliver?

1. ______________________________
2. ______________________________
3. ______________________________
4. ______________________________
5. ______________________________

Who do I need to reach out to today to make all this happen?

1. ______________________________
2. ______________________________
3. ______________________________
4. ______________________________
5. ______________________________

Daily Revenue Goal:

Actual:

End of day revenues:

Number of sales:

Daily Profit:

Daily Expenditures:

Sales in the pipeline:

Daily Capital/ Income Set Aside:

TODAY'S DATE: ______________________

MY DAILY TOP 5

Five things I am grateful for about my business and business finances right now.

1. ______________________
2. ______________________
3. ______________________
4. ______________________
5. ______________________

Who do I need to reach out to today?

1. ______________________
2. ______________________
3. ______________________
4. ______________________
5. ______________________

What do I need to do today to move me forward?
What are my IPA's for the day?

1. ______________________
2. ______________________
3. ______________________
4. ______________________
5. ______________________

What do I need to learn more about today to continue to grow and deliver?

1. ______________________
2. ______________________
3. ______________________
4. ______________________
5. ______________________

Who do I need to reach out to today to make all this happen?

1. ______________________
2. ______________________
3. ______________________
4. ______________________
5. ______________________

Daily Revenue Goal:

Actual:

End of day revenues:

Number of sales:

Daily Profit:

Daily Expenditures:

Sales in the pipeline:

Daily Capital/ Income Set Aside:

WEEK 3 REFLECTION

1. Did you hit your target weekly sales goal? .... [ ]
    a. No – how does that adjust next week's goal to stay on track for the month?
    b. Yes- Have a small celebration. This is a great start.

2. Are all bills due for this week paid?.. [ ]

3. All weekly transactions entered into your accounting system? .... [ ]

    This can be an actual accounting software or just a glorified check register kept in an Xcel spreadsheet, but it needs to be more than just verifying your bank account "looks right".

4. Did you pay yourself something for the week? .... [ ]

5. How much in the little expenses did you cut out this week? Was that easy for you or difficult? Why?

    ____

    ____

    ____

Weekly Revenue Goal:.............. [ ]   Actual:...................... [ ]

Budgeted Expenses:.................. [ ]   Actual: .... [ ]

Number of weekly sales: .... [ ]

Number of sales in the pipeline for next week: .... [ ]

Weekly Profit:.. [ ]

What amount did you pay yourself this week? .... [ ]

WEEK 4

"A big business starts small."

You are a quarter of the way to having created some amazing financial habits and wins in your business. Keep going, keep focused and don't stop now!

What are your needle movers?

What is a needle mover?

A needle mover is the thing or things that will have a big impact on the movement in your business.

A needle mover is the thing or things that will have a big impact on the movement in your business.

Focus on the financial needle movers.

Maybe you have been selling lots of small ticket items and have been putting off following up on that one big ticket client that could move your finances forward in a big way.

Lay out a plan for this week and reach out to them. The worst that can happen is they say no and you are still where you are at.... But if they say yes.....

WEEK 4 MINI-CHALLENGE

What are your top two or three needle movers to put focus on this week? Put a plan in place for those.

Needle Mover 1: ____________________

What is your plan? ____________________

____

____

____

Needle Mover 2: ____________________

What is your plan? ____________________

____

____

____

Needle Mover 3: ____________________

What is your plan? ____________________

____

____

____

TODAY'S DATE: ______________________

MY DAILY TOP 5

Five things I am grateful for about my business and business finances right now.

1. ______
2. ______
3. ______
4. ______
5. ______

Who do I need to reach out to today?

1. ______
2. ______
3. ______
4. ______
5. ______

What do I need to do today to move me forward?
What are my IPA's for the day?

1. ______
2. ______
3. ______
4. ______
5. ______

What do I need to learn more about today to continue to grow and deliver?

1. ______
2. ______
3. ______
4. ______
5. ______

Who do I need to reach out to today to make all this happen?

1. ______
2. ______
3. ______
4. ______
5. ______

Daily Revenue Goal:

Actual:

End of day revenues:

Number of sales:

Daily Profit:

Daily Expenditures:

Sales in the pipeline:

Daily Capital/ Income Set Aside:

TODAY'S DATE: ____________________

MY DAILY TOP 5

Five things I am grateful for about my business and business finances right now.

1. ____________________
2. ____________________
3. ____________________
4. ____________________
5. ____________________

Who do I need to reach out to today?

1. ____________________
2. ____________________
3. ____________________
4. ____________________
5. ____________________

What do I need to do today to move me forward?
What are my IPA's for the day?

1. ____________________
2. ____________________
3. ____________________
4. ____________________
5. ____________________

What do I need to learn more about today to continue to grow and deliver?

1. ____________________
2. ____________________
3. ____________________
4. ____________________
5. ____________________

Who do I need to reach out to today to make all this happen?

1. ____________________
2. ____________________
3. ____________________
4. ____________________
5. ____________________

Daily Revenue Goal:

Actual:

End of day revenues:

Number of sales:

Daily Profit:

Daily Expenditures:

Sales in the pipeline:

Daily Capital/ Income Set Aside:

TODAY'S DATE: ____________________

MY DAILY TOP 5

Five things I am grateful for about my business and business finances right now.

1. ____________________
2. ____________________
3. ____________________
4. ____________________
5. ____________________

Who do I need to reach out to today?

1. ____________________
2. ____________________
3. ____________________
4. ____________________
5. ____________________

What do I need to do today to move me forward?
What are my IPA's for the day?

1. ____________________
2. ____________________
3. ____________________
4. ____________________
5. ____________________

What do I need to learn more about today to continue to grow and deliver?

1. ____________________
2. ____________________
3. ____________________
4. ____________________
5. ____________________

Who do I need to reach out to today to make all this happen?

1. ____________________
2. ____________________
3. ____________________
4. ____________________
5. ____________________

Daily Revenue Goal:

Actual:

End of day revenues:

Number of sales:

Daily Profit:

Daily Expenditures:

Sales in the pipeline:

Daily Capital/ Income Set Aside:

TODAY'S DATE: ______________________

MY DAILY TOP 5

Five things I am grateful for about my business and business finances right now.

1. ______________________
2. ______________________
3. ______________________
4. ______________________
5. ______________________

Who do I need to reach out to today?

1. ______________________
2. ______________________
3. ______________________
4. ______________________
5. ______________________

What do I need to do today to move me forward? What are my IPA's for the day?

1. ______________________
2. ______________________
3. ______________________
4. ______________________
5. ______________________

What do I need to learn more about today to continue to grow and deliver?

1. ______________________
2. ______________________
3. ______________________
4. ______________________
5. ______________________

Who do I need to reach out to today to make all this happen?

1. ______________________
2. ______________________
3. ______________________
4. ______________________
5. ______________________

Daily Revenue Goal:

Actual:

End of day revenues:

Number of sales:

Daily Profit:

Daily Expenditures:

Sales in the pipeline:

Daily Capital/ Income Set Aside:

TODAY'S DATE: ____________________

MY DAILY TOP 5

Five things I am grateful for about my business and business finances right now.

1. ____________________
2. ____________________
3. ____________________
4. ____________________
5. ____________________

Who do I need to reach out to today?

1. ____________________
2. ____________________
3. ____________________
4. ____________________
5. ____________________

What do I need to do today to move me forward?
What are my IPA's for the day?

1. ____________________
2. ____________________
3. ____________________
4. ____________________
5. ____________________

What do I need to learn more about today to continue to grow and deliver?

1. ____________________
2. ____________________
3. ____________________
4. ____________________
5. ____________________

Who do I need to reach out to today to make all this happen?

1. ____________________
2. ____________________
3. ____________________
4. ____________________
5. ____________________

Daily Revenue Goal:

Actual:

End of day revenues:

Number of sales:

Daily Profit:

Daily Expenditures:

Sales in the pipeline:

Daily Capital/ Income Set Aside:

WEEK 4 REFLECTION

1. Did you hit your target weekly sales goal? ....
   a. No – how does that adjust next week's goal to stay on track for the month?
   b. Yes- Have a small celebration. This is a great start.
2. Are all bills due for this week paid?..........
3. All weekly transactions entered into your accounting system? ....

   This can be an actual accounting software or just a glorified check register kept in an Xcel spreadsheet, but it needs to be more than just verifying your bank account "looks right".
4. Did you pay yourself something for the week? ....
5. What was the outcome of focusing on your needle movers? Make needle movers a part of your weekly routin and set a couple for each and every week?

   ___

   ___

   ___

5. Are you still honoring your calendar time for financial tasks in your business?

   ___

   ___

   ___

Weekly Revenue Goal:.......... Actual:..........

Budgeted Expenses:.......... Actual: ....

Number of weekly sales: ....

Number of sales in the pipeline for next week: ....

Weekly Profit:..........

What amount did you pay yourself this week? ....

MONTH 1

Part of tracking your business finances successfully is monitoring financial trends and data.

Slow periods, peak periods, high and low spending periods. Do certain services or products sell more during a certain time of year than they do during the rest of the year.

Knowing these trends can help you plan out your marketing plan, can help you determine when to launch new offerings and have such an overall impact on the finance side of your business.

Remember to pay yourself this month- take actual money out of your business bank account and put it in your personal account!

MONTH 1 OPERATIONS

1. Did you hit your monthly targeted revenue and expenditure goals? ....

   a. Yes- congratulations! You are on your way to taking control of your finances and having the financial success you are capable of! Have a celebration of some sorts. Nothing big and expensive but do something special to celebrate.

   b. No- That is ok. Celebrate the fact that you know this. Now course correct. Why didn't you hit the goals?

      i. What were the bumps that prevented the goal from being reached and how will you plan to overcome them next month?

Bump: ______________________________

What is your plan? ______________________________

____

____

____

Bump: ______________________________

What is your plan? ______________________________

____

____

____

Bump: ______________________________

What is your plan? ______________________________

____

____

____

Ii. Adjust your next month's goal to include the shortfall from this month so you don't fall behind for the annual goal.

This Month's Shortfall .... [ ]

Plus: Next Month's Goal.. [ ]

Equals: Next Month's ADJUSTED goal.. [ ]

iii. Revisit your goal.

Based on the first month, is your goal
realistic based on your pricing?.. [ ]

If not, how can you adjust your price to reach your goal? Can you add in a bonus training or something small that allows the value to be maintained while still increasing your prices slightly to achieve your goals? Brainstorm some ideas on how you can add value here:

____

____

____

____

2. Look at next month's goals and break them down to your weekly and daily goals and map out your course to get there again this next month.

What is your profit goal for the month?.. [ ]

Break that out to a WEEKLY goal (monthly goal/4.3): .... [ ]

Break that out to a DAILY goal (weekly goal/5 working days): .... [ ]

MONTH 1 REVIEW

Week 1 Revenue Goal:............. [ ] Actual:..................... [ ]

Week 2 Revenue Goal:............ [ ] Actual:..................... [ ]

Week 3 Revenue Goal:............. [ ] Actual:..................... [ ]

Week 4 Revenue Goal:............. [ ] Actual:..................... [ ]

Week1 Expense Budget: .... [ ] Actual:..................... [ ]

Week2 Expense Budget: .... [ ] Actual:..................... [ ]

Week3 Expense Budget: .... [ ] Actual:..................... [ ]

Week4 Expense Budget: .... [ ] Actual:..................... [ ]

Week 1 Number of Sales:......... [ ] Week 1 Profit:......... [ ]

Week 2 Number of Sales:......... [ ] Week 2 Profit:......... [ ]

Week 3 Number of Sales:......... [ ] Week 3 Profit:......... [ ]

Week 4 Number of Sales:......... [ ] Week 4 Profit:......... [ ]

Now to take this a step farther, trends are super important to your business.

You can download a template to put these numbers into (final numbers only) to be able to see a trend for your revenues, expenses and profits at the end of this journal.

www.ElevatingProfits.com/Financially_Focused_Trends

WEEK 5

"The best successes come on the heels of failure."

By now you may have had a week where you didn't hit those goals you laid out financially for your business.

Don't let that derail you. Use it as motivation.

Maybe have more conversations to get the yesses you need. Maybe stay a little longer after the meeting is over to see who you can chat with. Maybe have one more call with a possible power partner this week- you never know what one thing may turn everything around.

You've got this! You are a month in. Habits are being formed.

Who do you need to talk to this week that could move your business forward in a HUGE way? Write their name down here and reach out to them before the end of the week.

Who is it? ______________________________

Why? ______________________________

When will you reach out? ______________________________

TODAY'S DATE: ____________________

MY DAILY TOP 5

Five things I am grateful for about my business and business finances right now.

1. ____________________
2. ____________________
3. ____________________
4. ____________________
5. ____________________

Who do I need to reach out to today?

1. ____________________
2. ____________________
3. ____________________
4. ____________________
5. ____________________

What do I need to do today to move me forward?
What are my IPA's for the day?

1. ____________________
2. ____________________
3. ____________________
4. ____________________
5. ____________________

What do I need to learn more about today to continue to grow and deliver?

1. ____________________
2. ____________________
3. ____________________
4. ____________________
5. ____________________

Who do I need to reach out to today to make all this happen?

1. ____________________
2. ____________________
3. ____________________
4. ____________________
5. ____________________

Daily Revenue Goal:

Actual:

End of day revenues:

Number of sales:

Daily Profit:

Daily Expenditures:

Sales in the pipeline:

Daily Capital/ Income Set Aside:

TODAY'S DATE: ______________________

MY DAILY TOP 5

Five things I am grateful for about my business and business finances right now.

1. ______________________
2. ______________________
3. ______________________
4. ______________________
5. ______________________

Who do I need to reach out to today?

1. ______________________
2. ______________________
3. ______________________
4. ______________________
5. ______________________

What do I need to do today to move me forward?
What are my IPA's for the day?

1. ______________________
2. ______________________
3. ______________________
4. ______________________
5. ______________________

What do I need to learn more about today to continue to grow and deliver?

1. ______________________
2. ______________________
3. ______________________
4. ______________________
5. ______________________

Who do I need to reach out to today to make all this happen?

1. ______________________
2. ______________________
3. ______________________
4. ______________________
5. ______________________

Daily Revenue Goal:

Actual:

End of day revenues:

Number of sales:

Daily Profit:

Daily Expenditures:

Sales in the pipeline:

Daily Capital/ Income Set Aside:

TODAY'S DATE: ______________________

MY DAILY TOP 5

Five things I am grateful for about my business and business finances right now.

1. ______________________
2. ______________________
3. ______________________
4. ______________________
5. ______________________

Who do I need to reach out to today?

1. ______________________
2. ______________________
3. ______________________
4. ______________________
5. ______________________

What do I need to do today to move me forward?
What are my IPA's for the day?

1. ______________________
2. ______________________
3. ______________________
4. ______________________
5. ______________________

What do I need to learn more about today to continue to grow and deliver?

1. ______________________
2. ______________________
3. ______________________
4. ______________________
5. ______________________

Who do I need to reach out to today to make all this happen?

1. ______________________
2. ______________________
3. ______________________
4. ______________________
5. ______________________

Daily Revenue Goal:

Actual:

End of day revenues:

Number of sales:

Daily Profit:

Daily Expenditures:

Sales in the pipeline:

Daily Capital/ Income Set Aside:

TODAY'S DATE: ______________________

MY DAILY TOP 5

Five things I am grateful for about my business and business finances right now.

1. ______
2. ______
3. ______
4. ______
5. ______

Who do I need to reach out to today?

1. ______
2. ______
3. ______
4. ______
5. ______

What do I need to do today to move me forward?
What are my IPA's for the day?

1. ______
2. ______
3. ______
4. ______
5. ______

What do I need to learn more about today to continue to grow and deliver?

1. ______
2. ______
3. ______
4. ______
5. ______

Who do I need to reach out to today to make all this happen?

1. ______
2. ______
3. ______
4. ______
5. ______

Daily Revenue Goal:

Actual:

End of day revenues:

Number of sales:

Daily Profit:

Daily Expenditures:

Sales in the pipeline:

Daily Capital/ Income Set Aside:

TODAY'S DATE: ______________________

MY DAILY TOP 5

Five things I am grateful for about my business and business finances right now.

1. ______________________
2. ______________________
3. ______________________
4. ______________________
5. ______________________

Who do I need to reach out to today?

1. ______________________
2. ______________________
3. ______________________
4. ______________________
5. ______________________

What do I need to do today to move me forward?
What are my IPA's for the day?

1. ______________________
2. ______________________
3. ______________________
4. ______________________
5. ______________________

What do I need to learn more about today to continue to grow and deliver?

1. ______________________
2. ______________________
3. ______________________
4. ______________________
5. ______________________

Who do I need to reach out to today to make all this happen?

1. ______________________
2. ______________________
3. ______________________
4. ______________________
5. ______________________

Daily Revenue Goal:

Actual:

End of day revenues:

Number of sales:

Daily Profit:

Daily Expenditures:

Sales in the pipeline:

Daily Capital/ Income Set Aside:

WEEK 5 REFLECTION

1. Did you hit your target weekly sales goal? ....
   a. No – how does that adjust next week's goal to stay on track for the month?
   b. Yes- Have a small celebration. This is a great start.

2. Are all bills due for this week paid?..

3. All weekly transactions entered into your accounting system? ....

   This can be an actual accounting software or just a glorified check register kept in an Xcel spreadsheet, but it needs to be more than just verifying your bank account "looks right".

4. Did you pay yourself something for the week? ....

5. How did the conversation with the person you needed to reach out to go?

   ____

   ____

   ____

7. Who else do you need to reach out to in order to reach your goal??

   Who is it? ____

   Why? ____

   When will you reach out? ____

Weekly Revenue Goal:.............. Actual:......................

Budgeted Expenses:.................. Actual: ....

Number of weekly sales: ....

Number of sales in the pipeline for next week: ....

Weekly Profit:...

What amount did you pay yourself this week? ....

WEEK 6

"Revenue is vanity, profit is sanity, but cash is king."

Unknown

If you have done any of my courses or watched any of my training videos, you know I value cash flow over profits.

Profits are important, but as I say, a business can operate without profits for years, a business without cash flow will fail in months.

Manage your cash flow.

Collect money that is owed to you and do all you can to not spend it all right away.

This week's focus is ensuring you have clear payment terms set with your clients and that they are clearly communicated.

Look at your contracts or agreements- are the payment terms and expectations clearly laid out?

Look at your accounts receivable, who owes you money? Reach out to those people and get paid what you are owed or stop the work immediately. If the work is already been done, set up a plan for you to ensure you are getting paid prior to completion or delivery.

TODAY'S DATE: ______________________

MY DAILY TOP 5

Five things I am grateful for about my business and business finances right now.

1. ______________________
2. ______________________
3. ______________________
4. ______________________
5. ______________________

Who do I need to reach out to today?

1. ______________________
2. ______________________
3. ______________________
4. ______________________
5. ______________________

What do I need to do today to move me forward?
What are my IPA's for the day?

1. ______________________
2. ______________________
3. ______________________
4. ______________________
5. ______________________

What do I need to learn more about today to continue to grow and deliver?

1. ______________________
2. ______________________
3. ______________________
4. ______________________
5. ______________________

Who do I need to reach out to today to make all this happen?

1. ______________________
2. ______________________
3. ______________________
4. ______________________
5. ______________________

Daily Revenue Goal:

Actual:

End of day revenues:

Number of sales:

Daily Profit:

Daily Expenditures:

Sales in the pipeline:

Daily Capital/ Income Set Aside:

TODAY'S DATE: ______________________

MY DAILY TOP 5

Five things I am grateful for about my business and business finances right now.

1. ______________________
2. ______________________
3. ______________________
4. ______________________
5. ______________________

Who do I need to reach out to today?

1. ______________________
2. ______________________
3. ______________________
4. ______________________
5. ______________________

What do I need to do today to move me forward?
What are my IPA's for the day?

1. ______________________
2. ______________________
3. ______________________
4. ______________________
5. ______________________

What do I need to learn more about today to continue to grow and deliver?

1. ______________________
2. ______________________
3. ______________________
4. ______________________
5. ______________________

Who do I need to reach out to today to make all this happen?

1. ______________________
2. ______________________
3. ______________________
4. ______________________
5. ______________________

Daily Revenue Goal:

Actual:

End of day revenues:

Number of sales:

Daily Profit:

Daily Expenditures:

Sales in the pipeline:

Daily Capital/ Income Set Aside:

TODAY'S DATE: ______________________

MY DAILY TOP 5

Five things I am grateful for about my business and business finances right now.

1. ______________________
2. ______________________
3. ______________________
4. ______________________
5. ______________________

Who do I need to reach out to today?

1. ______________________
2. ______________________
3. ______________________
4. ______________________
5. ______________________

What do I need to do today to move me forward?
What are my IPA's for the day?

1. ______________________
2. ______________________
3. ______________________
4. ______________________
5. ______________________

What do I need to learn more about today to continue to grow and deliver?

1. ______________________
2. ______________________
3. ______________________
4. ______________________
5. ______________________

Who do I need to reach out to today to make all this happen?

1. ______________________
2. ______________________
3. ______________________
4. ______________________
5. ______________________

Daily Revenue Goal:

Actual:

End of day revenues:

Number of sales:

Daily Profit:

Daily Expenditures:

Sales in the pipeline:

Daily Capital/ Income Set Aside:

TODAY'S DATE: ____________________

MY DAILY TOP 5

Five things I am grateful for about my business and business finances right now.

1. ____________________
2. ____________________
3. ____________________
4. ____________________
5. ____________________

Who do I need to reach out to today?

1. ____________________
2. ____________________
3. ____________________
4. ____________________
5. ____________________

What do I need to do today to move me forward?
What are my IPA's for the day?

1. ____________________
2. ____________________
3. ____________________
4. ____________________
5. ____________________

What do I need to learn more about today to continue to grow and deliver?

1. ____________________
2. ____________________
3. ____________________
4. ____________________
5. ____________________

Who do I need to reach out to today to make all this happen?

1. ____________________
2. ____________________
3. ____________________
4. ____________________
5. ____________________

Daily Revenue Goal:

Actual:

End of day revenues:

Number of sales:

Daily Profit:

Daily Expenditures:

Sales in the pipeline:

**Daily Capital/
Income Set Aside:**

TODAY'S DATE: ____________________

MY DAILY TOP 5

Five things I am grateful for about my business and business finances right now.

1. ____________________
2. ____________________
3. ____________________
4. ____________________
5. ____________________

Who do I need to reach out to today?

1. ____________________
2. ____________________
3. ____________________
4. ____________________
5. ____________________

What do I need to do today to move me forward?
What are my IPA's for the day?

1. ____________________
2. ____________________
3. ____________________
4. ____________________
5. ____________________

What do I need to learn more about today to continue to grow and deliver?

1. ____________________
2. ____________________
3. ____________________
4. ____________________
5. ____________________

Who do I need to reach out to today to make all this happen?

1. ____________________
2. ____________________
3. ____________________
4. ____________________
5. ____________________

Daily Revenue Goal:

Actual:

End of day revenues:

Number of sales:

Daily Profit:

Daily Expenditures:

Sales in the pipeline:

Daily Capital/ Income Set Aside:

WEEK 6 REFLECTION

1. Did you hit your target weekly sales goal? ....
   a. No – how does that adjust next week's goal to stay on track for the month?
   b. Yes- Have a small celebration. This is a great start.
2. Are all bills due for this week paid? ....
3. All weekly transactions entered into your accounting system? ....

   This can be an actual accounting software or just a glorified check register kept in an Xcel spreadsheet, but it needs to be more than just verifying your bank account "looks right".
4. Did you pay yourself something for the week? ....
5. How much were you owed from clients when you looked at your accounts receivable? ....
6. How much were you able to collect from past due accounts? ....
7. Did you make the adjustments to your contracts to ensure payment terms and expectations are extremely clear? ....

Weekly Revenue Goal: .... Actual: ....

Budgeted Expenses: .... Actual: ....

Number of weekly sales: ....

Number of sales in the pipeline for next week: ....

Weekly Profit: ....

What amount did you pay yourself this week? ....

WEEK 7

"You must gain control of your money or the lack of it will forever control you."

Dave Ramsey

No one likes the word budget- it makes us feel like we can't do something. So set a plan for your money – a plan of how much and where you will spend it. Yes, this is a budget, but looking at it this way may make it easier to operate within.

You have to tell your money where to go rather than letting it tell you what you can or can't do.

This week as revenue is coming in, I want you to spend a little bit of time allocating every dollar out. Don't forget to allocate some to your pay and some to profits.

TODAY'S DATE: ____________________

MY DAILY TOP 5

Five things I am grateful for about my business and business finances right now.

1. ____________________
2. ____________________
3. ____________________
4. ____________________
5. ____________________

Who do I need to reach out to today?

1. ____________________
2. ____________________
3. ____________________
4. ____________________
5. ____________________

What do I need to do today to move me forward?
What are my IPA's for the day?

1. ____________________
2. ____________________
3. ____________________
4. ____________________
5. ____________________

What do I need to learn more about today to continue to grow and deliver?

1. ____________________
2. ____________________
3. ____________________
4. ____________________
5. ____________________

Who do I need to reach out to today to make all this happen?

1. ____________________
2. ____________________
3. ____________________
4. ____________________
5. ____________________

Daily Revenue Goal:

Actual:

End of day revenues:

Number of sales:

Daily Profit:

Daily Expenditures:

Sales in the pipeline:

Daily Capital/ Income Set Aside:

TODAY'S DATE: ______________________

MY DAILY TOP 5

Five things I am grateful for about my business and business finances right now.

1. ______________________
2. ______________________
3. ______________________
4. ______________________
5. ______________________

Who do I need to reach out to today?

1. ______________________
2. ______________________
3. ______________________
4. ______________________
5. ______________________

What do I need to do today to move me forward?
What are my IPA's for the day?

1. ______________________
2. ______________________
3. ______________________
4. ______________________
5. ______________________

What do I need to learn more about today to continue to grow and deliver?

1. ______________________
2. ______________________
3. ______________________
4. ______________________
5. ______________________

Who do I need to reach out to today to make all this happen?

1. ______________________
2. ______________________
3. ______________________
4. ______________________
5. ______________________

Daily Revenue Goal:

Actual:

End of day revenues:

Number of sales:

Daily Profit:

Daily Expenditures:

Sales in the pipeline:

Daily Capital/ Income Set Aside:

TODAY'S DATE: ____________________

MY DAILY TOP 5

Five things I am grateful for about my business and business finances right now.

1. ____________________
2. ____________________
3. ____________________
4. ____________________
5. ____________________

Who do I need to reach out to today?

1. ____________________
2. ____________________
3. ____________________
4. ____________________
5. ____________________

What do I need to do today to move me forward?
What are my IPA's for the day?

1. ____________________
2. ____________________
3. ____________________
4. ____________________
5. ____________________

What do I need to learn more about today to continue to grow and deliver?

1. ____________________
2. ____________________
3. ____________________
4. ____________________
5. ____________________

Who do I need to reach out to today to make all this happen?

1. ____________________
2. ____________________
3. ____________________
4. ____________________
5. ____________________

Daily Revenue Goal:

Actual:

End of day revenues:

Number of sales:

Daily Profit:

Daily Expenditures:

Sales in the pipeline:

Daily Capital/ Income Set Aside:

TODAY'S DATE: ____________________

MY DAILY TOP 5

Five things I am grateful for about my business and business finances right now.

1. ____________________
2. ____________________
3. ____________________
4. ____________________
5. ____________________

Who do I need to reach out to today?

1. ____________________
2. ____________________
3. ____________________
4. ____________________
5. ____________________

What do I need to do today to move me forward?
What are my IPA's for the day?

1. ____________________
2. ____________________
3. ____________________
4. ____________________
5. ____________________

What do I need to learn more about today to continue to grow and deliver?

1. ____________________
2. ____________________
3. ____________________
4. ____________________
5. ____________________

Who do I need to reach out to today to make all this happen?

1. ____________________
2. ____________________
3. ____________________
4. ____________________
5. ____________________

Daily Revenue Goal:

Actual:

End of day revenues:

Number of sales:

Daily Profit:

Daily Expenditures:

Sales in the pipeline:

Daily Capital/ Income Set Aside:

TODAY'S DATE: ______________________

MY DAILY TOP 5

Five things I am grateful for about my business and business finances right now.

1. ______________________
2. ______________________
3. ______________________
4. ______________________
5. ______________________

Who do I need to reach out to today?

1. ______________________
2. ______________________
3. ______________________
4. ______________________
5. ______________________

What do I need to do today to move me forward?
What are my IPA's for the day?

1. ______________________
2. ______________________
3. ______________________
4. ______________________
5. ______________________

What do I need to learn more about today to continue to grow and deliver?

1. ______________________
2. ______________________
3. ______________________
4. ______________________
5. ______________________

Who do I need to reach out to today to make all this happen?

1. ______________________
2. ______________________
3. ______________________
4. ______________________
5. ______________________

Daily Revenue Goal:

Actual:

End of day revenues:

Number of sales:

Daily Profit:

Daily Expenditures:

Sales in the pipeline:

Daily Capital/ Income Set Aside:

WEEK 7 REFLECTION

1. Did you hit your target weekly sales goal? ....
   a. No – how does that adjust next week's goal to stay on track for the month?
   b. Yes- Have a small celebration. This is a great start.
2. Are all bills due for this week paid?..........
3. All weekly transactions entered into your accounting system? ....

   This can be an actual accounting software or just a glorified check register kept in an Xcel spreadsheet, but it needs to be more than just verifying your bank account "looks right".
4. Did you pay yourself something for the week? ....
5. Was every dollar of revenue accounted for in your business this week? ....

Weekly Revenue Goal:.......... Actual:..........

Budgeted Expenses:.......... Actual: ....

Number of weekly sales: ....

Number of sales in the pipeline for next week: ....

Weekly Profit:..........

What amount did you pay yourself this week? ....

WEEK 8

"You have to get comfortable with your money. Know your numbers and you will grow your numbers."

Amanda Kendall

Maybe you have never been "great" at numbers, maybe "math is not your thing".

Who cares?

You own a business; money has to be your thing and money is math. So, math is now your thing. At least a little bit.

With a little knowledge on your side and the right plan, you can do exponential things with your business. It all starts with knowing your numbers.

This week's little extra challenge is to look at your pricing. Look at your expenses. Determine if you pricing allows for profits and if not, adjust your pricing.

TODAY'S DATE: ____________________

MY DAILY TOP 5

Five things I am grateful for about my business and business finances right now.

1. ______________________________
2. ______________________________
3. ______________________________
4. ______________________________
5. ______________________________

Who do I need to reach out to today?

1. ______________________________
2. ______________________________
3. ______________________________
4. ______________________________
5. ______________________________

What do I need to do today to move me forward?
What are my IPA's for the day?

1. ______________________________
2. ______________________________
3. ______________________________
4. ______________________________
5. ______________________________

What do I need to learn more about today to continue to grow and deliver?

1. ______________________________
2. ______________________________
3. ______________________________
4. ______________________________
5. ______________________________

Who do I need to reach out to today to make all this happen?

1. ______________________________
2. ______________________________
3. ______________________________
4. ______________________________
5. ______________________________

Daily Revenue Goal:

Actual:

End of day revenues:

Number of sales:

Daily Profit:

Daily Expenditures:

Sales in the pipeline:

Daily Capital/ Income Set Aside:

TODAY'S DATE: ______________________

MY DAILY TOP 5

Five things I am grateful for about my business and business finances right now.

1. ______________________
2. ______________________
3. ______________________
4. ______________________
5. ______________________

Who do I need to reach out to today?

1. ______________________
2. ______________________
3. ______________________
4. ______________________
5. ______________________

What do I need to do today to move me forward?
What are my IPA's for the day?

1. ______________________
2. ______________________
3. ______________________
4. ______________________
5. ______________________

What do I need to learn more about today to continue to grow and deliver?

1. ______________________
2. ______________________
3. ______________________
4. ______________________
5. ______________________

Who do I need to reach out to today to make all this happen?

1. ______________________
2. ______________________
3. ______________________
4. ______________________
5. ______________________

Daily Revenue Goal:

Actual:

End of day revenues:

Number of sales:

Daily Profit:

Daily Expenditures:

Sales in the pipeline:

Daily Capital/ Income Set Aside:

TODAY'S DATE: ________________________

MY DAILY TOP 5

Five things I am grateful for about my business and business finances right now.

1. ____________________
2. ____________________
3. ____________________
4. ____________________
5. ____________________

Who do I need to reach out to today?

1. ____________________
2. ____________________
3. ____________________
4. ____________________
5. ____________________

What do I need to do today to move me forward?
What are my IPA's for the day?

1. ____________________
2. ____________________
3. ____________________
4. ____________________
5. ____________________

What do I need to learn more about today to continue to grow and deliver?

1. ____________________
2. ____________________
3. ____________________
4. ____________________
5. ____________________

Who do I need to reach out to today to make all this happen?

1. ____________________
2. ____________________
3. ____________________
4. ____________________
5. ____________________

Daily Revenue Goal:

Actual:

End of day revenues:

Number of sales:

Daily Profit:

Daily Expenditures:

Sales in the pipeline:

Daily Capital/ Income Set Aside:

TODAY'S DATE: ______________________

MY DAILY TOP 5

Five things I am grateful for about my business and business finances right now.

1. ______________________
2. ______________________
3. ______________________
4. ______________________
5. ______________________

Who do I need to reach out to today?

1. ______________________
2. ______________________
3. ______________________
4. ______________________
5. ______________________

What do I need to do today to move me forward?
What are my IPA's for the day?

1. ______________________
2. ______________________
3. ______________________
4. ______________________
5. ______________________

What do I need to learn more about today to continue to grow and deliver?

1. ______________________
2. ______________________
3. ______________________
4. ______________________
5. ______________________

Who do I need to reach out to today to make all this happen?

1. ______________________
2. ______________________
3. ______________________
4. ______________________
5. ______________________

Daily Revenue Goal:

Actual:

End of day revenues:

Number of sales:

Daily Profit:

Daily Expenditures:

Sales in the pipeline:

Daily Capital/ Income Set Aside:

TODAY'S DATE: ____________________

MY DAILY TOP 5

Five things I am grateful for about my business and business finances right now.

1. ____________________
2. ____________________
3. ____________________
4. ____________________
5. ____________________

Who do I need to reach out to today?

1. ____________________
2. ____________________
3. ____________________
4. ____________________
5. ____________________

What do I need to do today to move me forward?
What are my IPA's for the day?

1. ____________________
2. ____________________
3. ____________________
4. ____________________
5. ____________________

What do I need to learn more about today to continue to grow and deliver?

1. ____________________
2. ____________________
3. ____________________
4. ____________________
5. ____________________

Who do I need to reach out to today to make all this happen?

1. ____________________
2. ____________________
3. ____________________
4. ____________________
5. ____________________

Daily Revenue Goal:

Actual:

End of day revenues:

Number of sales:

Daily Profit:

Daily Expenditures:

Sales in the pipeline:

Daily Capital/ Income Set Aside:

WEEK 8 REFLECTION

1. Did you hit your target weekly sales goal? ....
   a. No – how does that adjust next week's goal to stay on track for the month?
   b. Yes- Have a small celebration. This is a great start.
2. Are all bills due for this week paid? ....
3. All weekly transactions entered into your accounting system? ....

   This can be an actual accounting software or just a glorified check register kept in an Xcel spreadsheet, but it needs to be more than just verifying your bank account "looks right".
4. Did you pay yourself something for the week? ....
5. Did you look at your pricing? Are you charging enough or did you take steps to increase your prices? ....

Weekly Revenue Goal: .... Actual: ....

Budgeted Expenses: .... Actual: ....

Number of weekly sales: ....

Number of sales in the pipeline for next week: ....

Weekly Profit: ....

What amount did you pay yourself this week? ....

MONTH 2

How are those trends looking?

Are you getting the hang of this daily finance management thing?

You are 2/3 of the way through the 12 weeks at this point. You have spent some time focused on expenses and revenue sources, you have looked at pricing and you are rocking out this money management thing by now.

If you feel like you still need some more tips and tricks and want some ongoing support and advice, I want to encourage you to join the Facebook group The Entrepreneurs Profit Corner. The entrepreneurs who have joined that group are getting weekly tips and help to grow their business through intention, come over and join us.

Oh, and don't forget to pay yourself this month!!

MONTH 2 OPERATIONS

1. Did you hit your monthly targeted revenue and expenditure goals? ....

    a. Yes- congratulations! You are on your way to taking control of your finances and having the financial success you are capable of! Have a celebration of some sorts. Nothing big and expensive but do something special to celebrate.

    b. No- That is ok. Celebrate the fact that you know this. Now course correct. Why didn't you hit the goals?

        i. What were the bumps that prevented the goal from being reached and how will you plan to overcome them next month?

Bump: ____________________

What is your plan? ____________________

____

____

____

Bump: ____________________

What is your plan? ____________________

____

____

____

Bump: ____________________

What is your plan? ____________________

____

____

____

Ii. Adjust your next month's goal to include the shortfall from this month so you don't fall behind for the annual goal.

This Month's Shortfall ....

Plus: Next Month's Goal..

Equals: Next Month's ADJUSTED goal...

iii. Revisit your goal.

Based on the first month, is your goal realistic based on your pricing?...

If not, how can you adjust your price to reach your goal? Can you add in a bonus training or something small that allows the value to be maintained while still increasing your prices slightly to achieve your goals? Brainstorm some ideas on how you can add value here:

____

____

____

____

2. Look at next month's goals and break them down to your weekly and daily goals and map out your course to get there again this next month.

What is your profit goal for the month?...

Break that out to a WEEKLY goal (monthly goal/4.3): ....

Break that out to a DAILY goal (weekly goal/5 working days): ....

MONTH 2 REVIEW

Week 1 Revenue Goal:.............. [ ] Actual:...................... [ ]

Week 2 Revenue Goal:............. [ ] Actual:...................... [ ]

Week 3 Revenue Goal:.............. [ ] Actual:...................... [ ]

Week 4 Revenue Goal:.............. [ ] Actual:...................... [ ]

Week1 Expense Budget: .... [ ] Actual:...................... [ ]

Week2 Expense Budget: .... [ ] Actual:...................... [ ]

Week3 Expense Budget: .... [ ] Actual:...................... [ ]

Week4 Expense Budget: .... [ ] Actual:...................... [ ]

Week 1 Number of Sales:......... [ ] Week 1 Profit:......... [ ]

Week 2 Number of Sales:......... [ ] Week 2 Profit:......... [ ]

Week 3 Number of Sales:......... [ ] Week 3 Profit:......... [ ]

Week 4 Number of Sales:......... [ ] Week 4 Profit:......... [ ]

Add these numbers to your trends spreadsheet you downloaded after week 4. Tracking trends is so important. It allows you to see where seasons may impact your business, holidays, family events, and life. It all plays a role, knowing the role it plays helps you plan for them.

www.ElevatingProfits.com/Financially_Focused_Trends

WEEK 9

"The secret to achieving true success is found in your daily routine"

Unknown

That's right. Daily routines are what create the habits of success. And you my friend, are eight weeks into some amazing daily routines around your business finances.

I bet you are already seeing the difference managing a few simple things can have in your business. The impact is there. The growth is happening. The understanding is coming easier.

Might I even venture to say you like the finance aspect of your business now?

Ok, maybe that is a little too far... but you know what is financially going on in your business and should be taking a regular paycheck of some sort at this time.

This week I want you to just remain focused on all that we have done over the last eight weeks, go back and look at the trends you have plugged into the worksheet. Look for patterns. Tie those patterns to anything that happened. Life happens, and sometimes it changes our focus, accept that and just acknowledge how that may have impacted your numbers.

TODAY'S DATE: ____________________

MY DAILY TOP 5

Five things I am grateful for about my business and business finances right now.

1. ____________________
2. ____________________
3. ____________________
4. ____________________
5. ____________________

Who do I need to reach out to today?

1. ____________________
2. ____________________
3. ____________________
4. ____________________
5. ____________________

What do I need to do today to move me forward?
What are my IPA's for the day?

1. ____________________
2. ____________________
3. ____________________
4. ____________________
5. ____________________

What do I need to learn more about today to continue to grow and deliver?

1. ____________________
2. ____________________
3. ____________________
4. ____________________
5. ____________________

Who do I need to reach out to today to make all this happen?

1. ____________________
2. ____________________
3. ____________________
4. ____________________
5. ____________________

Daily Revenue Goal:

Actual:

End of day revenues:

Number of sales:

Daily Profit:

Daily Expenditures:

Sales in the pipeline:

Daily Capital/ Income Set Aside:

TODAY'S DATE: ____________________

MY DAILY TOP 5

Five things I am grateful for about my business and business finances right now.

1. ____________________
2. ____________________
3. ____________________
4. ____________________
5. ____________________

Who do I need to reach out to today?

1. ____________________
2. ____________________
3. ____________________
4. ____________________
5. ____________________

What do I need to do today to move me forward?
What are my IPA's for the day?

1. ____________________
2. ____________________
3. ____________________
4. ____________________
5. ____________________

What do I need to learn more about today to continue to grow and deliver?

1. ____________________
2. ____________________
3. ____________________
4. ____________________
5. ____________________

Who do I need to reach out to today to make all this happen?

1. ____________________
2. ____________________
3. ____________________
4. ____________________
5. ____________________

Daily Revenue Goal:

Actual:

End of day revenues:

Number of sales:

Daily Profit:

Daily Expenditures:

Sales in the pipeline:

Daily Capital/ Income Set Aside:

TODAY'S DATE: ______________________

MY DAILY TOP 5

Five things I am grateful for about my business and business finances right now.

1. ______________________________
2. ______________________________
3. ______________________________
4. ______________________________
5. ______________________________

Who do I need to reach out to today?

1. ______________________________
2. ______________________________
3. ______________________________
4. ______________________________
5. ______________________________

What do I need to do today to move me forward?
What are my IPA's for the day?

1. ______________________________
2. ______________________________
3. ______________________________
4. ______________________________
5. ______________________________

What do I need to learn more about today to continue to grow and deliver?

1. ______________________________
2. ______________________________
3. ______________________________
4. ______________________________
5. ______________________________

Who do I need to reach out to today to make all this happen?

1. ______________________________
2. ______________________________
3. ______________________________
4. ______________________________
5. ______________________________

Daily Revenue Goal:

Actual:

End of day revenues:

Number of sales:

Daily Profit:

Daily Expenditures:

Sales in the pipeline:

Daily Capital/ Income Set Aside:

TODAY'S DATE: ______________________

MY DAILY TOP 5

Five things I am grateful for about my business and business finances right now.

1. ______________________
2. ______________________
3. ______________________
4. ______________________
5. ______________________

Who do I need to reach out to today?

1. ______________________
2. ______________________
3. ______________________
4. ______________________
5. ______________________

What do I need to do today to move me forward?
What are my IPA's for the day?

1. ______________________
2. ______________________
3. ______________________
4. ______________________
5. ______________________

What do I need to learn more about today to continue to grow and deliver?

1. ______________________
2. ______________________
3. ______________________
4. ______________________
5. ______________________

Who do I need to reach out to today to make all this happen?

1. ______________________
2. ______________________
3. ______________________
4. ______________________
5. ______________________

Daily Revenue Goal:

Actual:

End of day revenues:

Number of sales:

Daily Profit:

Daily Expenditures:

Sales in the pipeline:

Daily Capital/ Income Set Aside:

TODAY'S DATE: ____________________

MY DAILY TOP 5

Five things I am grateful for about my business and business finances right now.

1. ____________________
2. ____________________
3. ____________________
4. ____________________
5. ____________________

Who do I need to reach out to today?

1. ____________________
2. ____________________
3. ____________________
4. ____________________
5. ____________________

What do I need to do today to move me forward?
What are my IPA's for the day?

1. ____________________
2. ____________________
3. ____________________
4. ____________________
5. ____________________

What do I need to learn more about today to continue to grow and deliver?

1. ____________________
2. ____________________
3. ____________________
4. ____________________
5. ____________________

Who do I need to reach out to today to make all this happen?

1. ____________________
2. ____________________
3. ____________________
4. ____________________
5. ____________________

Daily Revenue Goal:

Actual:

End of day revenues:

Number of sales:

Daily Profit:

Daily Expenditures:

Sales in the pipeline:

Daily Capital/ Income Set Aside:

WEEK 9 REFLECTION

1. Did you hit your target weekly sales goal? ....
   a. No – how does that adjust next week's goal to stay on track for the month?
   b. Yes- Have a small celebration. This is a great start.
2. Are all bills due for this week paid? ....
3. All weekly transactions entered into your accounting system? ....

   This can be an actual accounting software or just a glorified check register kept in an Xcel spreadsheet, but it needs to be more than just verifying your bank account "looks right".
4. Did you pay yourself something for the week? ....
5. Did you notice any financial trends in your business? ....

   If so, what were those? Are they able to be adjusted or are they just a seasonal trend you need to be aware of?

   ____

   ____

   ____

Weekly Revenue Goal: .... Actual: ....

Budgeted Expenses: .... Actual: ....

Number of weekly sales: ....

Number of sales in the pipeline for next week: ....

Weekly Profit: ....

What amount did you pay yourself this week? ....

WEEK 10

"Entrepreneurs believe that profits are what matter most in a new venture. But profit is secondary. Cash flow is what matters most."

Peter Drucker

Focus on the cash you have in your business this week and ensuring you have cash going from one week to the next continuously. This is the true driver of being successful.

TODAY'S DATE: ____________________

MY DAILY TOP 5

Five things I am grateful for about my business and business finances right now.

1. ____________________
2. ____________________
3. ____________________
4. ____________________
5. ____________________

Who do I need to reach out to today?

1. ____________________
2. ____________________
3. ____________________
4. ____________________
5. ____________________

What do I need to do today to move me forward?
What are my IPA's for the day?

1. ____________________
2. ____________________
3. ____________________
4. ____________________
5. ____________________

What do I need to learn more about today to continue to grow and deliver?

1. ____________________
2. ____________________
3. ____________________
4. ____________________
5. ____________________

Who do I need to reach out to today to make all this happen?

1. ____________________
2. ____________________
3. ____________________
4. ____________________
5. ____________________

Daily Revenue Goal:

Actual:

End of day revenues:

Number of sales:

Daily Profit:

Daily Expenditures:

Sales in the pipeline:

Daily Capital/ Income Set Aside:

TODAY'S DATE: ______________________

MY DAILY TOP 5

Five things I am grateful for about my business and business finances right now.

1. ______________________
2. ______________________
3. ______________________
4. ______________________
5. ______________________

Who do I need to reach out to today?

1. ______________________
2. ______________________
3. ______________________
4. ______________________
5. ______________________

What do I need to do today to move me forward?
What are my IPA's for the day?

1. ______________________
2. ______________________
3. ______________________
4. ______________________
5. ______________________

What do I need to learn more about today to continue to grow and deliver?

1. ______________________
2. ______________________
3. ______________________
4. ______________________
5. ______________________

Who do I need to reach out to today to make all this happen?

1. ______________________
2. ______________________
3. ______________________
4. ______________________
5. ______________________

Daily Revenue Goal:

Actual:

End of day revenues:

Number of sales:

Daily Profit:

Daily Expenditures:

Sales in the pipeline:

Daily Capital/ Income Set Aside:

TODAY'S DATE: ______________________

MY DAILY TOP 5

Five things I am grateful for about my business and business finances right now.

1. ______________________
2. ______________________
3. ______________________
4. ______________________
5. ______________________

Who do I need to reach out to today?

1. ______________________
2. ______________________
3. ______________________
4. ______________________
5. ______________________

What do I need to do today to move me forward?
What are my IPA's for the day?

1. ______________________
2. ______________________
3. ______________________
4. ______________________
5. ______________________

What do I need to learn more about today to continue to grow and deliver?

1. ______________________
2. ______________________
3. ______________________
4. ______________________
5. ______________________

Who do I need to reach out to today to make all this happen?

1. ______________________
2. ______________________
3. ______________________
4. ______________________
5. ______________________

Daily Revenue Goal:

Actual:

End of day revenues:

Number of sales:

Daily Profit:

Daily Expenditures:

Sales in the pipeline:

Daily Capital/ Income Set Aside:

TODAY'S DATE: ____________________

MY DAILY TOP 5

Five things I am grateful for about my business and business finances right now.

1. ____________________
2. ____________________
3. ____________________
4. ____________________
5. ____________________

Who do I need to reach out to today?

1. ____________________
2. ____________________
3. ____________________
4. ____________________
5. ____________________

What do I need to do today to move me forward?
What are my IPA's for the day?

1. ____________________
2. ____________________
3. ____________________
4. ____________________
5. ____________________

What do I need to learn more about today to continue to grow and deliver?

1. ____________________
2. ____________________
3. ____________________
4. ____________________
5. ____________________

Who do I need to reach out to today to make all this happen?

1. ____________________
2. ____________________
3. ____________________
4. ____________________
5. ____________________

Daily Revenue Goal:

Actual:

End of day revenues:

Number of sales:

Daily Profit:

Daily Expenditures:

Sales in the pipeline:

Daily Capital/ Income Set Aside:

TODAY'S DATE: ____________________

MY DAILY TOP 5

Five things I am grateful for about my business and business finances right now.

1. ____________________
2. ____________________
3. ____________________
4. ____________________
5. ____________________

Who do I need to reach out to today?

1. ____________________
2. ____________________
3. ____________________
4. ____________________
5. ____________________

What do I need to do today to move me forward?
What are my IPA's for the day?

1. ____________________
2. ____________________
3. ____________________
4. ____________________
5. ____________________

What do I need to learn more about today to continue to grow and deliver?

1. ____________________
2. ____________________
3. ____________________
4. ____________________
5. ____________________

Who do I need to reach out to today to make all this happen?

1. ____________________
2. ____________________
3. ____________________
4. ____________________
5. ____________________

Daily Revenue Goal:

Actual:

End of day revenues:

Number of sales:

Daily Profit:

Daily Expenditures:

Sales in the pipeline:

Daily Capital/ Income Set Aside:

WEEK 10 REFLECTION

1. Did you hit your target weekly sales goal? ....
    a. No – how does that adjust next week's goal to stay on track for the month?
    b. Yes- Have a small celebration. This is a great start.
2. Are all bills due for this week paid?..........
3. All weekly transactions entered into your accounting system? ....

    This can be an actual accounting software or just a glorified check register kept in an Xcel spreadsheet, but it needs to be more than just verifying your bank account "looks right".
4. Did you pay yourself something for the week? ....
5. Were you able to end the week with a positive cash flow with which to go into next week? ....

Weekly Revenue Goal:.......... Actual:..........

Budgeted Expenses:.......... Actual: ....

Number of weekly sales: ....

Number of sales in the pipeline for next week: ....

Weekly Profit:..........

What amount did you pay yourself this week? ....

WEEK 11

"Cash flow is not bragging rights. It is financial freedom."

Grant Cardone

You are almost done with this 12 week journey.

Congratulations on sticking to it thus far but make sure you finish it out.

This week think about how you will continue to implement this in the day-to-day of your business. Do you need another journal? Do you need to just focus on these items daily on your own?

What is the next step that will ensure you keep at this and don't let the finance piece slip from being top of mind when you are done with this?

Figure out what that is and lay out a plan for success.

If you would like to talk about next steps on how to continue to grow your business financially and achieve a new level of understanding I would love to have a conversation with you around that and see how I can support you.

You can reach out to me at ***www.ElevatingProfits.com/contact*** and click on the link to schedule a time to talk.

TODAY'S DATE: ____________________

MY DAILY TOP 5

Five things I am grateful for about my business and business finances right now.

1. ____________________
2. ____________________
3. ____________________
4. ____________________
5. ____________________

Who do I need to reach out to today?

1. ____________________
2. ____________________
3. ____________________
4. ____________________
5. ____________________

What do I need to do today to move me forward?
What are my IPA's for the day?

1. ____________________
2. ____________________
3. ____________________
4. ____________________
5. ____________________

What do I need to learn more about today to continue to grow and deliver?

1. ____________________
2. ____________________
3. ____________________
4. ____________________
5. ____________________

Who do I need to reach out to today to make all this happen?

1. ____________________
2. ____________________
3. ____________________
4. ____________________
5. ____________________

Daily Revenue Goal:

Actual:

End of day revenues:

Number of sales:

Daily Profit:

Daily Expenditures:

Sales in the pipeline:

Daily Capital/ Income Set Aside:

TODAY'S DATE: ____________________

MY DAILY TOP 5

Five things I am grateful for about my business and business finances right now.

1. ____________________
2. ____________________
3. ____________________
4. ____________________
5. ____________________

Who do I need to reach out to today?

1. ____________________
2. ____________________
3. ____________________
4. ____________________
5. ____________________

What do I need to do today to move me forward?
What are my IPA's for the day?

1. ____________________
2. ____________________
3. ____________________
4. ____________________
5. ____________________

What do I need to learn more about today to continue to grow and deliver?

1. ____________________
2. ____________________
3. ____________________
4. ____________________
5. ____________________

Who do I need to reach out to today to make all this happen?

1. ____________________
2. ____________________
3. ____________________
4. ____________________
5. ____________________

Daily Revenue Goal:

Actual:

End of day revenues:

Number of sales:

Daily Profit:

Daily Expenditures:

Sales in the pipeline:

Daily Capital/ Income Set Aside:

TODAY'S DATE: ____________________

MY DAILY TOP 5

Five things I am grateful for about my business and business finances right now.

1. ____________________
2. ____________________
3. ____________________
4. ____________________
5. ____________________

Who do I need to reach out to today?

1. ____________________
2. ____________________
3. ____________________
4. ____________________
5. ____________________

What do I need to do today to move me forward?
What are my IPA's for the day?

1. ____________________
2. ____________________
3. ____________________
4. ____________________
5. ____________________

What do I need to learn more about today to continue to grow and deliver?

1. ____________________
2. ____________________
3. ____________________
4. ____________________
5. ____________________

Who do I need to reach out to today to make all this happen?

1. ____________________
2. ____________________
3. ____________________
4. ____________________
5. ____________________

Daily Revenue Goal:

Actual:

End of day revenues:

Number of sales:

Daily Profit:

Daily Expenditures:

Sales in the pipeline:

Daily Capital/ Income Set Aside:

TODAY'S DATE: ____________________

MY DAILY TOP 5

Five things I am grateful for about my business and business finances right now.

1. ____________________
2. ____________________
3. ____________________
4. ____________________
5. ____________________

Who do I need to reach out to today?

1. ____________________
2. ____________________
3. ____________________
4. ____________________
5. ____________________

What do I need to do today to move me forward?
What are my IPA's for the day?

1. ____________________
2. ____________________
3. ____________________
4. ____________________
5. ____________________

What do I need to learn more about today to continue to grow and deliver?

1. ____________________
2. ____________________
3. ____________________
4. ____________________
5. ____________________

Who do I need to reach out to today to make all this happen?

1. ____________________
2. ____________________
3. ____________________
4. ____________________
5. ____________________

Daily Revenue Goal:

Actual:

End of day revenues:

Number of sales:

Daily Profit:

Daily Expenditures:

Sales in the pipeline:

Daily Capital/ Income Set Aside:

TODAY'S DATE: ____________________

MY DAILY TOP 5

Five things I am grateful for about my business and business finances right now.

1. ____________________
2. ____________________
3. ____________________
4. ____________________
5. ____________________

Who do I need to reach out to today?

1. ____________________
2. ____________________
3. ____________________
4. ____________________
5. ____________________

What do I need to do today to move me forward?
What are my IPA's for the day?

1. ____________________
2. ____________________
3. ____________________
4. ____________________
5. ____________________

What do I need to learn more about today to continue to grow and deliver?

1. ____________________
2. ____________________
3. ____________________
4. ____________________
5. ____________________

Who do I need to reach out to today to make all this happen?

1. ____________________
2. ____________________
3. ____________________
4. ____________________
5. ____________________

Daily Revenue Goal:

Actual:

End of day revenues:

Number of sales:

Daily Profit:

Daily Expenditures:

Sales in the pipeline:

Daily Capital/ Income Set Aside:

WEEK 11 REFLECTION

1. Did you hit your target weekly sales goal? ....
   a. No – how does that adjust next week's goal to stay on track for the month?
   b. Yes- Have a small celebration. This is a great start.
2. Are all bills due for this week paid?............
3. All weekly transactions entered into your accounting system? ....

   This can be an actual accounting software or just a glorified check register kept in an Xcel spreadsheet, but it needs to be more than just verifying your bank account "looks right".
4. Did you pay yourself something for the week? ....
5. What does your next step after next week look like for you? Lay out your plan so that you have a road map on how to stay involved in your business finances to elevate your profits:

Weekly Revenue Goal:............ Actual:............

Budgeted Expenses:............ Actual: ....

Number of weekly sales: ....

Number of sales in the pipeline for next week: ....

Weekly Profit:............

What amount did you pay yourself this week? ....

WEEK 12

"It's simple arithmetic. Your income can grow only to the extent that you do."

T. Harveker

You have spent almost 12 weeks building this muscle in your business. Training it, developing it, pushing through even when you may not have felt like it.

Your business will grow from this.

Continue to learn in this area of business. Continue to learn in all areas.

Find a weakness and turn it into a strength.

TODAY'S DATE: ____________________

MY DAILY TOP 5

Five things I am grateful for about my business and business finances right now.

1. ____________________
2. ____________________
3. ____________________
4. ____________________
5. ____________________

Who do I need to reach out to today?

1. ____________________
2. ____________________
3. ____________________
4. ____________________
5. ____________________

What do I need to do today to move me forward?
What are my IPA's for the day?

1. ____________________
2. ____________________
3. ____________________
4. ____________________
5. ____________________

What do I need to learn more about today to continue to grow and deliver?

1. ____________________
2. ____________________
3. ____________________
4. ____________________
5. ____________________

Who do I need to reach out to today to make all this happen?

1. ____________________
2. ____________________
3. ____________________
4. ____________________
5. ____________________

Daily Revenue Goal:

Actual:

End of day revenues:

Number of sales:

Daily Profit:

Daily Expenditures:

Sales in the pipeline:

Daily Capital/ Income Set Aside:

TODAY'S DATE: ____________________

MY DAILY TOP 5

Five things I am grateful for about my business and business finances right now.

1. ____________________
2. ____________________
3. ____________________
4. ____________________
5. ____________________

Who do I need to reach out to today?

1. ____________________
2. ____________________
3. ____________________
4. ____________________
5. ____________________

What do I need to do today to move me forward?
What are my IPA's for the day?

1. ____________________
2. ____________________
3. ____________________
4. ____________________
5. ____________________

What do I need to learn more about today to continue to grow and deliver?

1. ____________________
2. ____________________
3. ____________________
4. ____________________
5. ____________________

Who do I need to reach out to today to make all this happen?

1. ____________________
2. ____________________
3. ____________________
4. ____________________
5. ____________________

Daily Revenue Goal:

Actual:

End of day revenues:

Number of sales:

Daily Profit:

Daily Expenditures:

Sales in the pipeline:

Daily Capital/ Income Set Aside:

TODAY'S DATE: ____________________

MY DAILY TOP 5

Five things I am grateful for about my business and business finances right now.

1. ____________________
2. ____________________
3. ____________________
4. ____________________
5. ____________________

Who do I need to reach out to today?

1. ____________________
2. ____________________
3. ____________________
4. ____________________
5. ____________________

What do I need to do today to move me forward?
What are my IPA's for the day?

1. ____________________
2. ____________________
3. ____________________
4. ____________________
5. ____________________

What do I need to learn more about today to continue to grow and deliver?

1. ____________________
2. ____________________
3. ____________________
4. ____________________
5. ____________________

Who do I need to reach out to today to make all this happen?

1. ____________________
2. ____________________
3. ____________________
4. ____________________
5. ____________________

Daily Revenue Goal:

Actual:

End of day revenues:

Number of sales:

Daily Profit:

Daily Expenditures:

Sales in the pipeline:

Daily Capital/ Income Set Aside:

TODAY'S DATE: ____________________

MY DAILY TOP 5

Five things I am grateful for about my business and business finances right now.

1. ____________________
2. ____________________
3. ____________________
4. ____________________
5. ____________________

Who do I need to reach out to today?

1. ____________________
2. ____________________
3. ____________________
4. ____________________
5. ____________________

What do I need to do today to move me forward?
What are my IPA's for the day?

1. ____________________
2. ____________________
3. ____________________
4. ____________________
5. ____________________

What do I need to learn more about today to continue to grow and deliver?

1. ____________________
2. ____________________
3. ____________________
4. ____________________
5. ____________________

Who do I need to reach out to today to make all this happen?

1. ____________________
2. ____________________
3. ____________________
4. ____________________
5. ____________________

Daily Revenue Goal:

Actual:

End of day revenues:

Number of sales:

Daily Profit:

Daily Expenditures:

Sales in the pipeline:

Daily Capital/ Income Set Aside:

TODAY'S DATE: ______________________

MY DAILY TOP 5

Five things I am grateful for about my business and business finances right now.

1. ____________________
2. ____________________
3. ____________________
4. ____________________
5. ____________________

Who do I need to reach out to today?

1. ____________________
2. ____________________
3. ____________________
4. ____________________
5. ____________________

What do I need to do today to move me forward?
What are my IPA's for the day?

1. ____________________
2. ____________________
3. ____________________
4. ____________________
5. ____________________

What do I need to learn more about today to continue to grow and deliver?

1. ____________________
2. ____________________
3. ____________________
4. ____________________
5. ____________________

Who do I need to reach out to today to make all this happen?

1. ____________________
2. ____________________
3. ____________________
4. ____________________
5. ____________________

Daily Revenue Goal:

Actual:

End of day revenues:

Number of sales:

Daily Profit:

Daily Expenditures:

Sales in the pipeline:

Daily Capital/ Income Set Aside:

WEEK 12 REFLECTION

1. Did you hit your target weekly sales goal? ....
   a. No – how does that adjust next week's goal to stay on track for the month?
   b. Yes- Have a small celebration. This is a great start.
2. Are all bills due for this week paid?..........
3. All weekly transactions entered into your accounting system? ....

   This can be an actual accounting software or just a glorified check register kept in an Xcel spreadsheet, but it needs to be more than just verifying your bank account "looks right".
4. Did you pay yourself something for the week? ....

Weekly Revenue Goal:.......... Actual:..........

Budgeted Expenses:.......... Actual: ....

Number of weekly sales: ....

Number of sales in the pipeline for next week: ....

Weekly Profit:..........

What amount did you pay yourself this week? ....

MONTH 3

You have got a handle on your business finances- you are in control and forging ahead. It is a habit you have created, but just because you have a handle on it, don't make the same mistake I did and stop giving it the focus it needs. Stay at it, you are on the path to a successful business for yourself.

Remember these three things:

1. Cash flow is the priority ALWAYS.
2. Pricing must account for profits.
3. A profitable business may happen by accident, but it won't last without intention.

MONTH 3 OPERATIONS

1. Did you hit your monthly targeted revenue and expenditure goals? ....

    a. Yes- congratulations! You are on your way to taking control of your finances and having the financial success you are capable of! Have a celebration of some sorts. Nothing big and expensive but do something special to celebrate.

    b. No- That is ok. Celebrate the fact that you know this. Now course correct. Why didn't you hit the goals?

        i. What were the bumps that prevented the goal from being reached and how will you plan to overcome them next month?

        Bump: ______________________________

        What is your plan? ______________________________

        ____

        ____

        ____

        Bump: ______________________________

        What is your plan? ______________________________

        ____

        ____

        ____

        Bump: ______________________________

        What is your plan? ______________________________

        ____

        ____

        ____

Ii. Adjust your next month's goal to include the shortfall from this month so you don't fall behind for the annual goal.

This Month's Shortfall ....

Plus: Next Month's Goal..

Equals: Next Month's ADJUSTED goal...

iii. Revisit your goal.

Based on the first month, is your goal realistic based on your pricing?..

If not, how can you adjust your price to reach your goal? Can you add in a bonus training or something small that allows the value to be maintained while still increasing your prices slightly to achieve your goals? Brainstorm some ideas on how you can add value here:

____

____

____

____

2. Look at next month's goals and break them down to your weekly and daily goals and map out your course to get there again this next month.

What is your profit goal for the month?..

Break that out to a WEEKLY goal (monthly goal/4.3): ....

Break that out to a DAILY goal (weekly goal/5 working days): ....

MONTH 3 REVIEW

Week 1 Revenue Goal:.............. [ ] Actual:...................... [ ]

Week 2 Revenue Goal:............. [ ] Actual:...................... [ ]

Week 3 Revenue Goal:.............. [ ] Actual:...................... [ ]

Week 4 Revenue Goal:.............. [ ] Actual:...................... [ ]

Week1 Expense Budget: .... [ ] Actual:...................... [ ]

Week2 Expense Budget: .... [ ] Actual:...................... [ ]

Week3 Expense Budget: .... [ ] Actual:...................... [ ]

Week4 Expense Budget: .... [ ] Actual:...................... [ ]

Week 1 Number of Sales:......... [ ] Week 1 Profit:......... [ ]

Week 2 Number of Sales:......... [ ] Week 2 Profit:......... [ ]

Week 3 Number of Sales:......... [ ] Week 3 Profit:......... [ ]

Week 4 Number of Sales:......... [ ] Week 4 Profit:......... [ ]

Add these to your trend sheet. Look at the trends over the last 12 weeks. If you continue to track these for a full year you will start to see how all that occurs in a year- holidays, vacation, seasons, school, etc. impacts the ebbs and flows of your business. Knowing this allows you to plan for success year round.

www.ElevatingProfits.com/Financially_Focused_Trends

CONCLUSION

"Financial freedom is a mental, emotional and educational process.."

Robert Kiyosaki

Congratulations! You did it, you spent 12 weeks, fully focused on your business finances.

Mentally you have fought through all your doubts of being able to manage the money in your business.

Emotionally you have faced areas where you didn't like what you saw or what you use to allow to happen.

Educationally you have learned better ways and new habits of taking control of the finances in your business.

I want you to take some time to reflect on these past 12 weeks.

How did it feel to be intentional around this part of your business?

Do you feel like you understand what is flowing into and out of your business on a regular basis now?

The next step is to keep at it! You can order another Financially Focused journal, or you can create your own system to track this information regularly.

The key is to track it. When you stop giving this part of your business attention, it will start to falter (I speak from experience on this).

Set up a system that works for you. Don't try to find the time to manage the expenses, make the time otherwise it won't happen. Make it an appointment with yourself.

Honor the hard work you put into your business. Pay yourself. Do it now! (Yes, that is me being slightly bossy.)

Make sure your pay comes as a priority to your business. Make sure you are paid for all the hard work you put in. Don't allow yourself to be an afterthought of the finances. Don't put everyone else before you. Your business would not exist if it were not for the hard work, long hours and dedication you put in. And in some cases, tears, lots of tears, sleepless nights and maybe a few panic attacks. Because of all this, you have earned a regular paycheck. Managing your finances is the first important step to getting one consistently.

ABOUT THE AUTHOR

Amanda Kendall, EA, is a business consultant with a background as a tax and accounting professional with over 16 years' experience. In 2012, Amanda established her first business which quickly catapulted to one of the top tax resolution firms with under 20 employees. Despite her focused and driven personality and a passion for helping her clients Amanda found herself personally struggling in her own business.

The experience and insight she gained from turning her business from near bankruptcy to being one of the most successful small businesses in her industry evolved into a desire to work with small business owners and service providers to create businesses that gave them the financial and time freedom they desired when they started their entrepreneurial journey. Thus, Elevating Profits, LLC was born.

As a business consultant and strategist, Amanda works with her clients to build a solid foundation based on four key factors, allowing them to create profit margins and freedom of time in a way that will be sustainable all while creating a business that is not reliant on their day to day presence.

Single mom to Liam and Daniel, Amanda currently lives in the North Denver suburb of Northglenn with her boyfriend, two sons, three dogs, and one cat where she enjoys taking advantage of the beautiful scenery that Colorado has to offer, by hiking and camping. She and her family also enjoy traveling and seeing new places, and escape to the beach whenever they can. Amanda is passionate about advocating for and helping single moms, volunteering her time to related organizations and activities whenever she can.

Amanda offers her consulting services to individuals and groups through one-on-one sessions, workshops and trainings, both in-person and online. She and her team at Elevating Profits, LLC provide growth and strategy consulting services along with CFO services to small- to medium-sized businesses and service providers throughout Colorado and the US.

Amanda has been an Enrolled Agent since 2011, passing all three parts of the stringent IRS test in just three months. She has been honored as a National Tax Practice Institute Fellow (2015), the National Association of Professional Women's (NAPW) Woman of the Year Award (2016), and the International Women's Leadership Association's (IWLA) Women of Outstanding Leadership Award (2016). A member of the Continental Who's Who association, Amanda was recognized as their Pinnacle Professional of the Year.

Made in the USA
Monee, IL
20 February 2020